THE FIRST DEPLOYMENT

INTERVIEWS AND INSPIRATION FOR THOSE WHO SUPPORT THE MILITARY

ANNA LUIKEN

New Harbor Press

RAPID CITY, SD

i

Luiken/New Harbor Press
1601 Mt. Rushmore Rd, Ste 3288
Rapid City, SD 57701
www.newharborpress.com

Ordering Information:
Quantity sales. Special discounts are available on quantity purchases by corporations, associations, and others. For details, contact the "Special Sales Department" at the address above.

The First Deployment/Luiken. -- 1st ed.
ISBN 978-1-63357-421-2

To the Girl Squads Around the World

And

To My Mom, Captain of the First Girl Squad I Was A Part Of

CONTENTS

ONE

YES, I REMEMBER IT

Yes, I remember it—looking into this baby's eyes and both loving her fiercely and fighting fiercely to continue loving her the right way, the way two parents present would, the way two parents should. There are the wishes and hopes, the shoulds and the woulds. But there is also the reality, the taking in of what is, the accepting of the difference between imagination and the here and now. Yes, I still remember it—the moment my sister-in-law shut the door and the baby I just brought home from the hospital fidgeting in her bouncer—the moment I felt truly alone and the wholeness of that feeling so entirely. My toddler, staring at the screen and I felt it—the dread and worry and exhaustion and fear settling in. Those couple of weeks before my husband was able to come home for a short paternity leave from deployment, I remember both very clearly and also in a blurry, blocked out, numb way. If I force myself to think of it—I can. One foot bouncing the baby, the other hand around my toddler reading bedtime stories. One baby sleeping on my chest in the carrier, chopping food on the cutting board for my toddler, trying not to bend too far over or make too many sudden movements so as to stop everything if the baby began to cry and try to figure out breastfeeding again.

Yes, the memories are there—tucked away forcefully but acutely present—the wave after wave of hurdles and obstacles, one cascading over the next as I try and fail repeatedly to attempt to grasp a handle on each one. Kneeling down to talk to my toddler about listening, about not dumping crackers on the floor, digging into the small amount of brain power reserves I had left to somehow find the words I should be saying that would help her rethink her actions. Begging, pleading, shushing, cuddling the tiny new to the world eyes to close again. Trying to use the electric breast pump so my breast milk supply doesn't run out. Trying to get the toddler outside so she doesn't get too much screen time. Trying to enjoy it joyfully so that the stress of her mother being preoccupied for most of the day for months on end is not something that affects her. Answering the door to a visitor—trying to remember what conversation is supposed to look like. Expressing gratitude even if the conversation didn't even halfway help me to de-stress. Offering snacks (what felt like endlessly). Offering toys (what felt like nonstop). Reading books so that my toddler has that special bond and is learning like other toddlers. Worrying about her development for a moment. Sitting for two minutes after bedtime. Did I eat today? Did I even take care of the afterbirth wounds? All of this alone. The love of my life in a different country—worlds away. A phone call is not even a guarantee that I will be able to talk through all my emotions with him. That is, if I can even put words to the emotions I'm feeling.

Giving birth to a baby without my husband and caring for a baby and a toddler without him for almost eleven months (and multiple trainings before and after) is part of my story. It completely obliterated me emotionally, physically, and mentally. It ripped me open and tore me up. But with every wound there is a healing and a scar. And with every scar, a visible reminder of your body and heart's resilience and ability to repair.

The First Deployment

Maybe birth and a toddler and the parenting littles stage is not part of your journey currently. I wrote this book with the desire that the words would offer some wisdom for the different life stages one might be in during a deployment. For me, this book is about that scar, that visible reminder. I can run my hands over that scar and share the story now. It doesn't feel entirely healed but it doesn't hurt to touch either.

Sometimes I needed to cry. Sometimes I was mad, bitter, angry, frustrated. Sometimes I wished someone, anyone could help with the endless bath times and nap times and mealtimes. Someone else to cut carrots for the thousandth time. Someone else to discipline the tantrums. Sometimes I felt like I couldn't complain because good military wives can't do that.

For me, deployment looked like not remembering if I changed my underwear or the last time I showered. It looked like frozen pizzas and mac 'n' cheese out of the box and the easiest meals I could possibly make. It looked like the baby crying, toddler screaming, dish breaking on the floor, just found out we missed a FaceTime call moments. There was the epic tantrum from my two-year-old that ended in me crying on the front porch feeling like my emotional bank was completely spent. There was the moment when the deployment was extended because of COVID and I ran to the store, surrounded by faces full of fear and panic and shelves of food emptied. Or, maybe deployment for me was just the million mundane moments in between the crash and burn ones: the lonely and fearful nights when the thoughts seemed at their worst, the routine that you do over and over but just without your person, the big lump in your throat when you take that half-second to grieve the loss of the person you love not being physically present in your day-to-day life.

There is no guidebook or right words for these moments. But I can offer this: six women who have done it before, who have walked similar shoes. I chose to interview women who experienced military life in different ways. Two women interviewed are veteran spouses who have experienced twenty-five plus years of military life. One friend shares her perspective on a husband deploying right after marriage. Another friend is in the think of it, parenting three babes with a husband who is currently serving in the military. Another friend shares perspective on her past life of twelve years of taking on deployments with young children. One friend interviewed is currently in the middle of a deployment, working part-time and taking care of her infant son.

I share their stories along with bits and pieces of my own in the hope that it will help in the journey of your own story. I wanted to create this as if you are sitting down for coffee, listening to a friend. After I finished one of these interviews, I thought: "Why didn't I do this sooner? Why didn't I sit down with those who had done this before, listening, learning, plucking these bits of knowledge from these gems of women?"

My hope is that you may find encouragement in their sharing. I found these women whose interviews I conducted separately to have intertwined words of strength and bravery, woven together in shared experience. Their wisdom, their powerful ability to gather their families into fighting their own battles each day, their honesty and their humility have moved me deeply. They, like me, have felt at times weary and worn, ragged. But their stories remind me of the beauty of humanity. And that sometimes after the raw brutality of sacrifice, upon investigation, you may find yourself a new person with new characteristics on the other side of that sacrifice, a person who surprises you with their quiet confidence, boldness and unfettered ability to take on challenges. That pain cuts deep and sharp but it can also bring healing and wholeness, a renewal of the best parts of yourself and your family, a renewal worth fighting for.

TWO

INTERVIEW ONE: PRAYER AND OREOS

This friend is down-to-earth, hilarious, oh so real, and relatable. She was my first interview. I ended our time together in tears, having shared some of my deep-down thoughts and fears—the ones I didn't say out loud during the deployment because I didn't want others to judge me. She helped me pick up the pieces of those thoughts and bring them back to truth.

ANNA: How long was your family in the military and how many stations were you assigned to?

FRIEND: Twelve years, six stations during that time. One station was six years. The first three kids we had my husband was deployed when each kid was six weeks old.

ANNA: Were there certain military-given resources you utilized?

FRIEND: It was hard because family readiness was only available at certain times.

2014 was our last real deployment. We didn't have FaceTime back then. Only Skype. We emailed because there was not enough money to buy a laptop. We had to email videos of the kids.

ANNA: What makes deployment hard?

FRIEND: It doesn't matter if you have FaceTime. The thing that made it hard fifty years ago is still the same. Here's why:

sometimes it feels like it's pointless. It feels like it's about career advancement. The guys are in a country where no one wants us. The guys are playing Xbox or reading. War is terrible—at first, you think it's about the constitution or helping serve America but then it's just pointless. We will never not be at war again. The "war on terror" is the same war. It used to be that evil was so easy to see. But with soldiers now there is not a clear enemy. Maybe you feel like there's a bigger purpose, but sometimes it feels like nothing was accomplished. I can't tell them "muster up and do a good thing because you're serving your country" because if that's your hope, it can't be. Our hope is found in Jesus.

Someone got a promotion because they wore more reflective gear than someone else. It's hard because we would be in a spouse meeting and they would say things like: "Families are the first priority." I felt like I couldn't even sit through the meeting. What did they want me to do? Raise my hand and say: "You said the mission is crucial, but you don't have the right parts for the equipment on the plane." I just want them to be honest and say what they truly want: "My goal is to get one star." I was never good at the spouse's meetings; it felt like a funeral with everyone crying. It felt like a facade—it felt like they didn't really want to help families.

ANNA: What is the solution?

FRIEND: The solution is speaking to the heart of those families. Changing circumstances doesn't help people. Changing their hearts by knowing Jesus does.

ANNA: What was your worst or hardest moment on deployment?

FRIEND: Once on deployment, we all got a flu bug. I went to check on my kids. My kid on the bottom bunk threw up on my feet and I looked up and the kid on the top bunk threw up on my face. I was the only one there, so I had to clean it all up. Then I went to bed and I threw up.

Also, before automated water payments, my kids were five, three, one, and a newborn. My husband was deployed. The kids were getting up continually, so I went to my parents' house. The water bill came but we weren't there because we were at my parents'. When we got home, there was a power notice and the water was turned off saying we had a "delinquent account." It was 111 degrees outside so inside the house was 130 degrees. I went to the store and tried to use a power of attorney and the company didn't understand it. I started having a nervous breakdown—just the feeling of helplessness overwhelmed me. Eventually, they turned it back on for me.

Other hard moments were when either one of us felt alone or unwanted. Sometimes I felt like we were inconveniencing him (called at a bad time, etc.). I think it's okay to have those moments but, maybe, try telling each other: "You seem busy, let's try back another time." Simply put, the hardest thing looking back is you're apart.

Another hard thing for me is I would stay up until 2:00 a.m. because I didn't want to fall asleep alone.

Deployments can destroy marriages, but it doesn't have to. If there is pain in deployment, then guard that: that is good. It doesn't mean forget it and give up on your marriage; it means there is something you are longing for. You weren't meant to be separated.

ANNA: What were your best moments on deployment?

FRIEND: When I was serving other people. When I would stop thinking about myself. When my husband was gone, I would serve in the nursery at church because I was sad sitting in church alone. It was important to me to do that at least once a month: to serve other people.

ANNA: What were some ways you supported your husband while he was gone?

FRIEND: I would think about our day as a family and send details as if he were there throughout the day or moments we thought about him. For example: "You would be really proud of how our son did his math." I thought about how my husband might handle a situation in that moment and it changed how I handled it.

Sometimes my husband didn't feel like we needed him, and he didn't feel connected so taking the time to email him about the day made him see how much we thought about him. We were taking the time to be intentional. For example, we might say: "We sat looking at the moon and it was a really special moment." I would think about things that I wish we could share or moments that literally I wish he were standing next to me. Write an email like your loved one cares what you have to say. Believe that they do even when you feel like it isn't true. Start with the assumption that they care for you and believe that they are for you.

Pretend you have interesting things to say—like when you were dating. For example: "I read this in the news and I disagreed with it—I would love to hear your thoughts." There is an app called Instapaper and my husband and I created two separate accounts. It was like I was curating a newspaper. He makes mine and I make yours—a newspaper you each can read and comment on later. It could be anything: A disturbing Twinkie that defied science. Current events. Weird Al Yankovich. The Gospel Coalition. A con man coming to know Jesus. We can look at what each other posted and then that night we can talk about the articles.

When you are apart, you don't have the physical presence or physical chemistry in your relationship. I sometimes felt like I was utterly uninteresting or that sex was what makes me interesting. But when we are appreciating each other's minds and personalities, we are engaging the whole time with all parts of each other, and I can feel that he likes all the parts of me.

We would also send him packages and drawings from the kids. I tried to give him the opportunity to still shepherd me. If I had a question, I would ask him. He missed that—that feeling of still being needed.

Another way I tried to include him and support him is actively spending time thinking about him. I would tell him if I remembered a hike and why it was good. He really missed that kind of thing. My husband would say that is one of the hardest parts of deployment: that he wanted to know I was spending time thinking about him. Try remembering things they have said, how they think, and include them in how you go about your day. Share this with them when you can. For example: "Remember that plant you said I would kill? It did die."

I would also ask for his counsel on things but not on time-sensitive things (Example: Can I sign the kids up for soccer?). Sometimes, he couldn't get back to me in time and then we were both frustrated. I want him to be part of decisions, but if it is time sensitive, I would make a decision quickly.

ANNA: What advice would you give for the predeployment season?

FRIEND: Get a power of attorney. Make love to your husband. Pray together regularly before they leave. Put aside your pride. This is not a time to insist on being right. Make goals for deployment so you can say this time was fruitful. You could each have a goal for something to memorize. For the person staying at home, make goals so that you feel like you've achieved something and are reaching milestones. For example: read a certain book or have dinner with a friend. Now that your husband is gone, think of things you couldn't do when he was gone. Put something on the calendar and have something lined up every week to do- this helps the time go so much faster.

Come up with a deployment budget that's different from a normal budget. For example, establish that you might get $300 extra every month to use on fun things such as lattes or pizza. A lot of postdeployment problems have to do with finances and it is not fair to have that conversation while they are gone. Have conversations like how do we get to money not in our checking account and how much is okay to take out or if our car breaks down—where do I get money for this type of expense?

ANNA: Do you have any postdeployment advice?

FRIEND: Also make love to your husband. Let go of expectations of the postdeployment season and give them space. I should have done more like say: "Go connect with someone for a bike ride." His struggles can be not feeling community around him when he gets back. You, as the person back home, may have been having that community while he was gone but not him. My husband would have long years of not feeling like people really knew him. The reality is you've had some community and he has had zero.

ANNA: How do you help the kids support their dad during this time?

FRIEND: I would help the kids write emails or take them out and while doing it, I would say: "Dad wanted to surprise you with McDonald's." Remind them he is thinking about them and it is special because dad misses them. We would have him read books before he left and video or record it. There are dolls you can get with the deployed person's picture on it. Do countdowns—with the military, dates always change but you can add a paper chain and, when the kids are sleeping, add more or take away some so that it is more accurate as the time gets closer.

ANNA: What would be your biggest advice to someone about to face their first deployment or just a deployment in general?

FRIEND: Ask for help! Ask for help ahead of time because when you do need it, you don't want to. I used to say: "There is nothing Oreos and Coke can't fix." Make a "favorites" list and give it to all your friends. Write down your favorite drink/ restaurant/ store so that others know how to surprise you and care for you. You can't be ashamed that you can't do it by yourself. We need each other. It's not "cheating" to ask for help.

Once, during deployment, I was pregnant and sitting in my car drinking milk and eating Oreos. It was one of those rare moments to myself after a trip to the store. I looked over and the person in the next car was staring at me through the car window. I'd been caught. I opened the car door so the person could see my pregnant belly. The person nodded. She understood. Prayer is good, but sometimes Oreos are good.

ANNA: I have felt so guilty over not feeling like my kids are getting the best—that they are getting less than parenting because it's just me and there's simply not enough me to go around. What would you say about this?

FRIEND: I know what my husband would say: "It's cute that you think they get the best when we are BOTH there." What we have to give, one parent or two, it is never enough. Never "the best". Call on our community and call on Christ. What a beautiful picture for our kids to see- that Christ and others love them, even in their not enough-ness.

Our hope is not in being a good mom or in parenting as a good team. Our best parenting is when we recognize our weakness and allow our kids to see Jesus working. Deployment doesn't make us insufficient. It reveals our ever-present insufficiency. In this way, a deployment can be our greatest gift if we are willing to call out to Jesus and confess we need Him. For the Christian, calling out to God for help isn't a great admission of defeat. It is the first battle in a war that has already been won.

End of Interview

As she and I talked, I realized that maybe sometimes I thought God was saying: "You're ruined. You called on me." But my friend helped me to see that it's not like that. Instead, God says: "You called on me. I'm with you. I haven't left you. I'm with you in the dark and the worst and the hard. I'm with you in the spilled Cheerios and the baby crying on the plane and everyone staring and the feeling like no one gets it. I see you and I'm here." It's not about being good enough. It's about being weak enough to know who the truly good enough one is.

As my friend and I finished our conversation, I was struck by the power of saying out loud what I felt were some of my darkest thoughts. I had never put a voice to those fears—my worries about my kids having only one parent—and it felt so relieving to have them out in the open. There was a barrier in my mind (What would others say if they knew those thoughts?) and I had lifted the barrier to find myself wondering why I had placed it in the first place.

THREE

THE HIDDEN HAIR

If there is anything that "well-child checks" are for, it is for making parents feel that their child is the opposite of well. I once took my daughter Eila in for her three-month well-child check, my two year old trailing slowly, ever so slowly behind me in the doctor's office hall. During the appointment, we took Eila's clothes off to get her weighed and measured only for me to notice that one of her toes looked completely purple. Looking closer, I found that one of my own hairs had become wrapped around her toe so tightly that the blood flow was beginning to be cut off, the hair cutting deeper and deeper into her skin. The doctor and nurses immediately began buzzing around, finding tweezers and scissors, magnifying lenses, and working to remove the hair. I sat there, in shock: How could this have happened? How could this baby who I spent all my time with, day in and day out, caring for her every possible need, her cries and her hunger and her diapers and her sleep, how could she all along amidst that care have a blaring, bursting, bleeding need?

The toe felt like a representation of the deployment to me. What else had been hiding unnoticed from my sight, breaking down, dying, on the edge of its end?

Those are the emotions of deployment—parenting alone and parenting with fervor and having moments where you see so clearly what you can't do, what you've missed, what you simply cannot accomplish. The reservoir of inadequacy and independence building simultaneously, your hard shell of toughness hammered down to bits when your amount of need becomes unmistakably unignorable.

Here are some snippets of real life from deployment for me:

- My husband only having certain times to talk on the phone which happens to often be the worst possible times for me (baby crying, toddler tantrums) . . . not always . . . but the time difference can make it hard sometimes
- Checking the news worrying and then checking myself for worrying and telling myself to trust God with my husband's life. I had to learn: You can't live your life in fear, it cripples joy and true living.
- Holding the baby crying late at night, wishing for relief, wishing for my partner in crime/best friend/love
- Checking the mail would give me uncertainty and dread at times—Would there be mail that I wouldn't know what to do with financially or I wouldn't understand? (Yes, there often was.) The mail felt like one extra thing I had to do, another checklist item only I could do.
- Wanting to call family or friends but feeling like I could never truly talk because I was also having to watch the kids and attend to their needs—my phone calls with those I really needed support from felt distracted and scattered
- Watching your babies meet milestones, wishing my husband could see them (Christmas, birthdays, everyday things like eating solids or learning shapes and colors or crawling)

- Feeling the burden of caring for your home and keeping your family together with your main man gone (things around the house breaking, finances, kids doctor appointments, kids being sick)
- Torn between wanting to hold it together positively when talking to my husband so he doesn't worry about us but also wanting to share honestly so he can walk with us in the hard

I often felt that work helping others energized me and took me out of my own self-pity. As a counselor, I work with kids who have been through trauma and abuse. Workdays for me sometimes look like helping a child who is suicidal to work through their thoughts and be able to stabilize. Some days look like leading a group on body image or bullying or dating with a group of high-school girls.

I have a distinct memory from deployment of spending an entire day exhausted from parenting solo- trudging forward putting Band-Aids on invisible hurts to sweeping up endless crumbs to pushing the swings at the park to holding my youngest daughter who as my husband now puts it: "cries at her own existence." Later that afternoon, I went to work leading a therapy group with the boys at our facility, which led to one boy throwing a chair at me. I do not take personal what the kiddos I work with do. They have horrendous childhoods. But I do work to love them well, to give them the best of me in the best way I can and to show them an adult who cares. On this particular instance, I eventually had to take steps to have this child transported from our facility as his behavior escalated to the point of not being able to keep himself or others safe (a threshold we struggle with every day at my job). He started throwing chairs at me and grabbing onto anything he could to hurt everyone around. I had to have the other children go into their rooms so that they wouldn't be hurt. I took all the steps

I could to talk him down from his rage, using counseling skills I had been taught and all the best of me I could muster.

As I left that night and another counselor took over, I drove home to pay the babysitter and begin the process of dinner and bedtime—two things that each individually felt like huge feats of strength and accomplishment and took buckets of energy I did not think I could possibly have.

I took deep breaths as I drove. Adrenaline rushed through me—having just faced a child who wanted to hurt me out of his own hurt, who didn't have the eyes to see that the pain he felt wasn't my fault, but I was just the person in front of him that could help him take it on and process it. I found it difficult in the time of my husband's deployment to ask for others to watch my kids. Counseling kids who come from backgrounds of abuse or trauma, who need love and attention and care, felt like the best possible reason to spend time away from my own kids, the best reason to have some time and space away. But sometimes the sheer laughable ridiculousness of it all could not be ignored. Here I was—a working mom whose work took so much out of me, working a job with skyrocketing turnover rates, a mom to two littles who would not see their father for eleven months, a mom who would handle their wails and whimpers and whines from sunup to sundown and then, because I had a newborn who grew to a nine month old in the time my husband was gone, would also handle the hungry and sleepy needs while the sun was down.

Well-meaning family, friends, or acquaintances would ask that dreaded question that I both hoped for and hated: "How are you?" How do I even begin? Do I even try to answer honestly? Where would I start even if I DID answer honestly? How much time did they have? An hour? And did they want to watch my kids for me while I actually did try to answer? Oh, yeah, okay, probably not.

The First Deployment

Sometimes, I wanted to stay here: in the thought of how stupid hard deployment was. You could stay in it—the hard and the suck of the hard, the all-encompassing brutal, unrelenting hard. But when I did, the thoughts got darker and darker. How could I, like the kid who threw the chair, like the purple toe, not ignore the pain but process it, examine it, and begin to heal? How could I see deployment differently? I needed to work this question in my head, wring it out, wrestle with it, flip it around. I needed to ask others and I needed to ask myself.

FOUR

INTERVIEW TWO: ONLY SNAIL MAIL

This veteran mama and wife is very dear to me. She has walked through the deep pits and the high mountains with me. She has graciously pointed me back to my way when I was lost in those pits. She is strong, fiercely passionate, and loyal. I am honored to share her story with you.

ANNA: How long were you in the military?

FRIEND: Twenty-nine years.

ANNA: How many stations have you been to?

FRIEND: Seventeen total—the first one was when we were married for four or five years. The entire assignment, he would deploy for three weeks and then work from our home station for six weeks. The second overseas assignment was when he went to Desert Storm. On that one, he left in November and came home in March.

ANNA: What were your best moments or memories during a deployment?

FRIEND: Kids create a different dynamic. Advances have now been made to be more connected. During Desert Storm, we only had snail mail to stay connected. The biggest thing I learned early on was to connect with other military spouses who were also lonely. On holidays, we shared time together—especially with being overseas.

One of the most beautiful things was the relationships built with other people who had loved ones deployed—but that did require effort. Sometimes, you want to hide in your house counting down the days but finding others going through the same thing was helpful to me. Those people turned out to be my lifetime friends. The biggest thing that helps you through deployment is finding others. Finding a church home wherever we were was important to us too.

ANNA: What were some of your hardest moments or hardest memories during a deployment?

FRIEND: It's hard before your spouse leaves because the person deploying starts to check out early. There can be a lot of fighting. A coping mechanism for spouses might be to be mad—it can be easier to say bye when you are mad. If you have kids, try your hardest to make the last days great. He or she is trying to let go smoothly and has lots of emotions.

Communication was hard. Now you can FaceTime. One of our hardest times was when my husband sent me a letter every day but somehow they got lost. At one time, all members of the unit wrote letters home, but my husband didn't because he figured I had been receiving my letters every day that he had already sent. I went to an event and a soldier came back early and he brought letters for everyone except me and I had not received the other letters my husband had sent. I thought something was wrong or our relationship was over. We definitely had to work through that time and I later found out he had written to me every day.

I remember when one of my daughters didn't even know who her dad was when he came back after deployment. Now, with FaceTime, you can see faces but back then we didn't have that.

Some of the hardest things can be insecurities over marriage. Loneliness can be an unfaithful friend. You can get to a bad place.

ANNA: Do you have any advice for someone about to go through a deployment for the first time?

FRIEND: Find people that you can plug into and get to know— this makes you step outside your own pain and your own loneliness. The more you focus on the pain and loneliness, the more it is harmful to you. When you focus on something other than yourself, you are able to stop thinking about your own misery. It helps you combat your loneliness. See what needs others have and help them. Look at others and other families as being more needy than yourself. Think of others as needing more help than yourself. It can be really good for kids to see that too.

Also, enjoy life with your kids. Try to keep doing pizza nights or other weekly routines. Having a routine when you have kids is security for them, especially during a deployment. It's easy to stay up late or not get sleep, but it is helpful to get plenty of rest, create regular bedtimes, and set a regular bedtime for yourself. When you are tired, you don't do as well. It's tempting not to but routine is best.

ANNA: Do you have any advice for the predeployment season?

FRIEND: Talk about things you are going to do when daddy gets back, such as taking a fun family trip. This gives everyone a fun thing to look forward to.

We did use paper chains as countdowns to when he would come back—tearing off the links, getting smaller and smaller. Take a picture of them near the chain to celebrate how far you have come. You are able to say things like: "Look it's gotten smaller."

ANNA: Do you have any advice for during deployment?

FRIEND: We would have their dad send the kids handwritten letters. We can have all this technology, but I personally think having handwritten things from the person who is deployed can be so important—no matter how technology spreads. They will love looking at them and read them over and over.

ANNA: Do you have any advice for after deployment?

FRIEND: There are so many expectations when they come home. You've settled into a groove and a way of doing things and it feels like they have messed that routine up or are fighting that routine. You have to learn to step back and learn to let them lead in the home again. But, sometimes, the spouse can come back in and see things that aren't going well or aren't healthy and can give you advice on that. I think it is also important for spouses to have time alone together.

ANNA: What are some of your thoughts or memories from during deployment?

FRIEND: Sometimes, the soldiers come home and feel minimized and feel like they don't count. They feel not important. Let them express feelings. You were just in survival mode, just to get by, but once they come home, we need to allow them to be the head of our home again. Kids can sense tension.

Sometimes we can have anger on our part. We might think when they get home: "Wait a second, you don't get to come in and change things up!" It is okay to work through those feelings. We might feel like asking: "Are you questioning me?" But it is about learning to not throw back in their face that they were gone.

You don't want your kids to see you paralyzed. You want them to see you pressing on. Let your kids know that there is always someone worse than us. It is easy to focus on your hardships but show your kids how you serve others less fortunate—the homeless, the hurting, those in need.

ANNA: Did you feel like military resources were helpful?

FRIEND: Family Readiness Group—offer your help. This takes time and energy but takes your mind off of yourself.

The First Deployment

ANNA: What are your thoughts on accepting help during deployment, especially if you don't want to?

FRIEND: You're hurting yourself by having that mindset. When my son was acting up, I once asked another dad to come talk to him. This other dad ended up putting him to bed and helped with disciplining him. That made a statement to my son. You have to be in a place of humility to ask for help. If you don't want to ask for help, you are hurting your kids too.

End of Interview

I have lived much life with this friend and personally seen the "lifetime friends" she referred to in action. These friends had asked the hard questions and found answers together: How do we keep our kids educated when we move several times a year? Let's try home school. How do we tackle the stress of our husbands being gone? Let's let the kids play together while we talk out the stress. These were women who have literally been through war and peace, love and loss, and terrors and triumphs together. They had sewed up the tattered squares of the quilt of their families over the years with patience and gentle love. The military hadn't broken their drive, it had created it. Their sheer brawn had been drawn out in the solidarity of pushing forward together: another station, another move, another new place, another government tussle that will be fought by those they lifted up from home. This interview had me thinking about my future: What might my friendships look like years down the road? Will I have chosen to share life with those going through similar struggles? I hoped so, but I also knew as my friend said "that did require effort."

FIVE

ENTERING INTO OUR MESS

Before deployment, there is a part of me that truly believed I had it all together. "I will conquer this deployment"—I think, maybe I truly believed this before deployment started. Social media screams at us to flaunt our put-together lives, outfits, jobs, parenting methods. This can be even harder to stomach during deployment. You finally sit down for five minutes to yourself and find yourself scrolling on social media—you can easily convince yourself that everyone else has smiling, happy babies who sleep through the night, the perfect Christmas jammies or families that never have conflict. Those comparison feelings can creep in—Why can't I keep the house clean? Why can't I ever find time to curl my hair like this person? Why can't I handle these tantrums better? Why don't I have as good of friends as this other person does (clearly pictures show how a person can have the best friendships)? And then, the realization of inability becomes prominent. But the truth is this—no one has it all together. No one always wears the perfect outfit or has the perfect kids or perfect job or house or marriage. Believing that life is perfect is believing a lie.

Deployment cemented the truth: I am a mess. Deployment or not, I am not perfect. My original thoughts that "I will conquer

25

this deployment" quickly made way to the ever-present truth that deployment was conquering me.

Mess can be all-consuming. Those lies can be too. What if someone sees me like this? What if someone actually knows what is really going on in our marriage? What if someone sees how much TV my kids actually watch? What if someone sees how I yelled at my kids?

Well, what if?

What if . . . your inability, your mess, your immense amount of need, helps you see those who truly love you and want to help? What if . . . the mess brings you to see more of who you truly are . . . mess and achievements and failures and dreams and all? What if . . . the mess brings you closer to your creator, the God of the universe, a God desperate to know you but your facade of conquering wouldn't allow true relationship with the one truly able to conquer?

The beautiful, needed what if.

Dear friends, don't do it. Don't let mess, in the emotional or physical sense, keep you from letting others in during deployment (or nondeployment) life. Often, we only want to invite others in when we feel our homes are clean and our lives are put together and others can see the "best" parts of our lives. But people feel most comfortable when we share the entirety of our lives—it reminds us we are all human. It reminds us that there is one greater than us all who is able to conquer, one who loves us, mess and all. We can come fully, mess fully intact, to God.

I needed others so much on this deployment. Many saw the mess in our lives. Yes, the physical mess—dirty dishes, toys everywhere, laundry piled high. But also, the mess of my sin, my anger, the mess of parenting a toddler and a baby, the mess of my need and my weakness and my inability to do it all.

But that feeling—"I will conquer this deployment"—still felt attainable. That feeling that I so desperately want to make my life look perfect to others—a clean house, children that behave, a put-together meal, a "got it together" marriage, or a career I am rocking. It can be exhausting. Why do I do this?

Lots of reasons I think, but mostly maybe I am afraid of:

1. Admitting to myself that none of those things are perfect And

2. Showing others those things aren't perfect.

The irony is I often think that, maybe, others will like me more if I show them the perfect side of me; but, in life and especially deployment, I've found such deeper friendships and bonds formed in the imperfect—women laughing over our imperfections, celebrating that we don't have it all together but we can run to someone who can heal us and help us, someone who is perfect (Jesus). I found that the more I opened up about the hardest parts of what I was going through with others, the more honest others would share in return and the more authentic our relationships became.

Yes, we would laugh over coffee or tea, loving someone in their entirety, sin and all, committing to someone in marriage can be crazy hard. Yes, we would agree, over charcuterie boards or fresh muffins, kids drain all your energy from you and then ask for more while you are still sucking for oxygen. Yes, we would admit over a glass of wine, there are Cheerios and goldfish stuffed around my car that have now become fossilized.

Invite others over when the trash is still high, stinking from rotten bananas. Invite others over when you still haven't worked out or cleaned the toilet or scrubbed that pan with the cheese caked on it from two days ago. Because we need each other, and we need to see that we all aren't perfect. Don't let mess keep you from connecting. Don't let mess allow your loneliness to overtake you.

Do the opposite of what the world does—admit your weakness. No, this does not feel good—it feels vulnerable and risky and scary. However, it has POWER. It invites God into your life and heart and soul and mind. It allows you to see your need for Him. It allows others to see your need for Him and also their need for Him. It allows others to unite in the common thread of: We all need each other. We can't do this alone. We can conquer this deployment—with help from others and with a reliance on God.

"But he said to me, 'My grace is sufficient for you, for my power is made perfect in weakness.'" (2 Corinthians 12:9)

As we share the reality of how bad it is, how painful it is, how overwhelming it is, others are invited to step in on our behalf to help us. Our community increases and we can begin to visually see God working through others. God meets us there in our sincerity. The more we shout and share our weakness, the more we can begin to know God and the more we open up ourselves to be truly known.

SIX

INTERVIEW THREE: THE NORMAL
LITTLE THINGS

This friend is the one who responded to a 5:00 a.m. text message I sent when I was doubled over in pain from a bladder infection during deployment. She spent the night two Halloweens in a row when I was alone because, like a kid, I hate being alone at night on Halloween. She met me in my needs and explained that it was okay and good to share my needs. She understood those needs because she had been there herself as a military spouse.

ANNA: Do you have specific advice for someone dating, engaged, or as a married couple separated during deployments?

FRIEND: Sometimes, I felt like people forgot about me—it was just me and the dog. For me, the best thing I did was to pursue my own passions and hobbies. For example, I downhill skied a lot. I felt like it was a good time to bond with other women and ladies that didn't have a spouse who I might not hang out with as much if my spouse were home. Singles don't want to be the third wheel but, with him gone, I was able to give them more time.

In retrospect, I wish I could have asked for more help. Sometimes, I felt like I had to prove I was an independent woman, but I wish I could have learned to get over my pride or need to prove I can do it on my own. My other advice would be just not comparing—not comparing yourself to other single women or other spouses.

ANNA: How long were you in the military and how many stations?

FRIEND: My husband went to West Point for four years, so that was a five-year commitment and he had to be in the Army for five years. He graduated in May, and I met him four or five months after West Point and we started dating a couple months after that. Officially, we have had four-and-a half years together in the Army but now he is in the Army National Guard.

ANNA: What helped you prepare predeployment?

FRIEND: I didn't have months to prepare to like most people— the Army gave us three weeks' notice. We worked on logistics like writing his will. Our car got stolen in the weeks before he deployed and we had to deal with that as well. I didn't get to prepare a lot mentally and emotionally because it was a surprise. Normally, for other times away, when we had more of a heads-up, we would try to spend intentional time together. I wanted intentional time but I also didn't want to monopolize that time. We would try to spend a weekend together but I also wanted to give him time to spend with friends.

ANNA: What helped you stay connected during deployment?

FRIEND: We talked as much as we could—but that can be hit or miss, for example, if he had little to no cell service. Afghanistan has bad Internet, and the Internet wouldn't work. Sometimes I would keep notes in my phone like a funny little story that I could share with him later. When he was deployed, I did care packages, but mostly it was communicating and sharing about everyday life. It is helpful to still talk about the "normal little things" and not put so much pressure on the time you do get to talk. Trying to use multiple sources can help, so sometimes Facebook Messenger or whatever Wi-Fi allows.

ANNA: What advice would you give to someone facing a first deployment?

FRIEND: Know that it is a lot harder than you think it is—even if you've done shorter times away before. Set aside time for you. Know that it is okay to be upset. You don't have to put on a brave face.

I think there is a fine line between identifying as a military spouse and understanding your spouse's job. A job shouldn't be our identity, even if it is our own job; but, definitely, don't find your identity in your significant other's job—be your own person outside of your job or your spouse's job.

Be open to what the military does have to offer for support. Sometimes, I wrote it off but there are some good things to it. Don't be consumed with it but be open to the resources. Before the deployment, try to set up some kind of support—like these are some friends I can call or I don't really want to cook, these are some options—and have your support system in place before they leave.

ANNA: How did you handle the postdeployment time period?

FRIEND: A big thing for us was that a month before he came home, we would be talking about expectation management. Because, in my mind, we would be spending ten days together so we would have to talk about expectation management beforehand. For example, understanding he may be jet-lagged—he may need to sleep in. Try to talk about in a "perfect world" what postdeployment will look like versus realistically what postdeployment will look like. I had a list of projects but being realistic helps. Know that it will be difficult for the first days or weeks.

ANNA: What were some of your best moments during deployment?

FRIEND: I had a couple of moments of "I did this on my own" and seeing what I was capable of. I rebuilt a gate that blew down in the wind. There were some special moments that I planned while he was deployed—I got to see his family and my family. We went to Hawaii with his family, which was a different way to build a relationship with his family, even though he was gone, and we got to FaceTime with him while we were all together. Being able to countdown and being able to say: "We are in the last month!" or "We are in the last week" felt good.

ANNA: What were some of the hardest things during the deployment?

FRIEND: The things I had to deal with on my own—the gate getting blown down or the car got stolen before he left. We had a checkbook stolen and some fraudulent checks were written. I tried calling him to help but, with the time difference, he was asleep and I had to deal with it. The bank didn't handle it and the person emptied our account. So, I would say two things: (1) really big stuff I had to deal with on my own or (2) the little things I wanted to tell him but I couldn't always tell him when I wanted— those were the hardest things to face.

ANNA: What advice would you give for how to accept help during a deployment?

FRIEND: It can be hard to ask for help, especially if you are new to a location. For example, when I first moved here and he left, I didn't know anyone—so trying to get to know people around you before your loved one leaves is important in building relationships so you can ask for help if needed. Ask yourself if it is your pride getting in the way of asking for help because 98% of the time it's pride that keeps us from asking for help. Our culture prides itself on independence. Sometimes, you can do it on your own but it's a lot harder. It doesn't have to be something big to ask for help.

ANNA: Do you have any advice for holidays?

FRIEND: Fly to be with family on those days. That way, you can still have family traditions—or plan fun things with friends.

ANNA: Is there anything I missed that you would want to share?

FRIEND: I would say talking about military life in general. Two weeks after we got married, he was gone for two weeks with ability for connection. A lot of people say to find things in common for marriage but, actually, I think it is good to find some hobbies you love and it is okay to have separate hobbies. It is good to find things to do together, but you don't have to only pursue shared interests. For example, living in Alaska, I learned to cross-country ski and hike. I learned to do things when he is home and pursue those passions so that when he is gone I can have something to do and look forward to. The military can be all-consuming but it is okay to have your own hobbies.

ANNA: Are there any military resources you would recommend?

FRIEND: Use the FRG, or Family Readiness Group, resources. There is also The Blue Star Program—dedicated to families with deployed family members. For example, they had an event called "Sips N Strokes" where you sip a drink and paint a picture. Don't feel bad utilizing the freebies they give to deployed spouses. Living on base can be nice. If you are living on base and your spouse is deployed here in Alaska, they shovel for you or do yardwork. Another recommendation is to utilize free child care for spouses.

End of Interview

This friend had me laughing—her sharing stories of fixing things herself and there was that instant bond—we knew what it was like to tackle projects we never would have tried before deployment. Those projects had helped us see our independence but also our isolation. It took guts to ask for help. We both knew this. This friend helped me confront notions about my identity as a woman, wife, and a military spouse. What does it look like to know myself during deployment? What does it look like to be supportive of my husband and his job while also being my own person? I was beginning to find answers to these questions, to know myself. But I needed to keep going. These are needed questions with needed answers.

SEVEN

WE MISSED HIM

We missed him. His big broad shoulders and his strong arms that play wrestle and how only he can do the voices in certain bedtime stories. I missed him when both girls were losing it and I had no extra hands. I missed him when the baby smiled and kicked and clasped my finger for the first time and I had no one to share it with.

My heart would sometimes ache when I saw dads holding their babies in carriers and kissing them on their heads in the store. My husband didn't get to do that with our youngest daughter, Eila. She spent most of her first nine months with me. Yes, he gets it now (when he is home) and I am thankful for that. But he missed a lot. And it hurt a lot. I tried to block out emotions sometimes, simply out of a need to emotionally survive. I felt I only had so much in my emotional bank and had to protect it to have enough to care for my girls and myself. I couldn't let myself think about the hard. "Survival mode" many people call it. But as someone who has a counseling degree I know, this isn't the healthiest or best choice. If you don't let it out, it will force itself out. When you least expect it. Like when you see a dad kissing his baby in the store, clearly taking his babe on a little dad–daughter date. Or when someone posts a picture of their family, complete with dad and baby together. All of a sudden, the tears and the emotions and all the true stuff, the stuff blocked behind barriers, come out.

What do you do with this weight, this heavy heartache, this burden that feels unbearable at times? This is a question I asked during deployment and, if I would be honest, I still ask as time away from the person we love is still a reality we face every day currently.

For me, the answer was to see the goodness God has for me in the moment. Cry out to God in the hard. Let it be okay to not be okay. Find someone you really trust to share the hard with. Allow others to step into the roles you can't fill. Yes, our baby didn't get my husband for the first nine months of her life. But while she didn't get my husband, we had a crew of dads from church who held her, loved her, calmed her, snuggled her. She had her Gramps, my husband's dad. She had uncles. She had real aunties (by blood) and adopted aunties (my friends) who loved her and loved us in a million ways I could never even count. She wasn't forgotten. Let the good be real and true (others loving her) just as much as the crying out to God in the hard (her not having her dad) can be real and true.

EIGHT

THE GIFT

The Christmas Tony was deployed he had bought Jemma, our two-year-old at the time, a Christmas present. In the midst of all the Christmas traditions, this gift seemed like all that mattered.

On Christmas Day, I wanted her to open this present first. I called Tony and he didn't answer. How could he not answer? It is Christmas Day—the biggest family event of the year. Yes, I knew there was a time difference, and he was maybe at dinner or about to go to bed. But it didn't matter. He missed this huge moment. Finally, I set aside this gift and Jemma opened others. Tony called back in the middle of the madness. I tried to explain to Jemma how Tony had sent this gift and how much we missed him and how he picked out this gift for her. But the moment was tense— she was distracted, focused on watching her cousins, on playing, on just being a kid at Christmas.

I kept forcing the screen in her face, taking away from her enjoying the moment and the gifts from others. Emotions started bubbling up. She was frustrated, I was frustrated, he was frustrated. All those thoughts started creeping in: Why can't we be a normal family? Why can't we have a family Christmas together? Why can't he just be here instead of halfway across the world?

There was so much pressure for her to react a certain way, for her to love that present the best and for her to show him how excited and thankful she was. I didn't realize how much pressure I had put on her but it was there, boldly trying to claim the entirety of the day.

I had put so much pressure on Tony—to make the fact that he was gone this Christmas right, to make FaceTime work as a communication tool, to answer his phone when I called, to make me feel that it was going to be alright, that he was going to come back, that even though we didn't get to be together on a day that felt so important to be together didn't mean our kids were doomed.

Where I went wrong was the making of feelings. The forcing of feelings. The necessity of my own idea of perfection, of family, of what it should be like instead of what it was.

At my work, we say often: "No one can make you angry." Often, when we act a certain way, we want to blame—"He made me do it." But the way we act is a choice. Our feelings aren't often a choice. They are what they are: feelings. Feelings aren't right or wrong or good or bad. But they can teach us about ourselves and give us a choice. We get a choice with what to do with our feelings.

With Tony on this Christmas Day, I felt angry. I felt angry that our Christmas was so different. Comparison amplifies discontentment. *"Why can't we be like other families at Christmas?"* This question isn't helpful because it doesn't bring solutions in the moment. We don't have Tony at holidays or birthdays or special moments sometimes. But I have to remind myself of truth when my thoughts begin to unravel out of control. I can choose to be angry or choose to remind myself of truth and let that truth wash over me, my feelings, my thoughts, no matter what is going on around me. The truth is Tony loves us, he would be there if he could and he will be there for other holidays. The truth is our family doesn't have to look like other families, we are what we are (and I love who we are), and we can choose to make the best of what we have.

We have a choice with anger. We can give in and choose to let it overtake the day, to dwell on it and live in it and let it eat away and rot our insides. Or we can talk to our partners about these feelings, to work on small, practical answers that might not fully mend the frustration but can help. We can celebrate the small things. We can say "I understand" when we realize that deployment for our loved ones means they have to balance work, connecting even with time zone differences and missing their own families.

I did talk to Tony that day about how I wished it had been different and how I felt like I was holding onto so much emotion the whole day. It felt good to share my true feelings and he did understand, he did miss us, he did want to be there. We didn't have a solution—"Maybe next time we can do a private phone call after we all open presents" or "Maybe we can schedule ahead better next time"—but we could say: "Let's keep working on it." We didn't know what the next time would bring or what our desires might be in those moments. All we knew was that we learned what didn't work and we were willing to put in the effort to keep trying to show each other love for the future.

I am an extrovert. I have been on the extreme, at times very extreme, side of extroverting in my life. When I worked as a full-time teacher before I had kids, I had something socially planned every night of the week in addition to the weekends (church small group, Bible study, youth group) in addition to the necessary duties of teaching, grading, coaching, etc.

I had this idea that people filled me up, met my needs, made me happy. In a lot of ways they had—many, many times in my life. I made people laugh, I could relate to people, I could help people, I loved people. Then came deployment.

Deployment stripped me of my free time to socialize, my ability to take a break because my partner came home to take over, my ability to allow people or extroverting be a thing I could regularly engage with. Deployment brought trying to wrangle two kids by myself to go to any social situation and then trying to have a conversation that was somewhat genuine while also trying to chase two kids during said conversation. Social situations, what used to be one of my very favorite things in the world, were now not as energizing or as fun as they used to be.

When I first had Eila and many people saw my need—a newborn and husband deployed—I remember several people with good intentions promising to help out with chores around the house or hire housework help or help with yardwork or just help in general. Some of those promises never came through. This wounded me in the sense that I had believed in people. People rarely disappointed me. But now, they had. Big time. In the moments I needed them most.

But two seemingly opposite things can be true at the same time: The very worst thing that could have happened on deployment was that people didn't meet all my needs and the very best thing that could have happened on deployment was that people didn't meet all my needs. These two rivaling facts brought me to my knees in desperate prayer and in desperate confusion. I was stripped of all ability to rely on anything or anyone but God. Deployment brought to the forefront, where I could deny it no longer, how much expectation, how much hope I had placed on people around me meeting my needs instead of God.

The truth became so clear: My everything can't be my therapist, my pastor, my favorite podcaster, my friend, my free time or gym time. It can't be my husband or my kids—as much as they DO feel like my everything at times. I can't put all that on any one person. No one person can give me all that I need.

The First Deployment

Ultimately, people have disappointed and failed me at times. They will continue to. Because they were never meant to meet all my needs! As a person who is a self-appointed people pleaser or people person like me, this came as news to me. The idea that people couldn't supply my every need was shocking and saddening—they had given me so much in life, so seeing the lack left a void.

To be clear, especially to anyone reading who was there for me during deployment, in many ways, a thousand times over, people were there for me on deployment, but my heart had been set on people (not God) meeting all my needs at times. But no one person or group of people could ever meet all of my needs all of the time. What ruined me was the expectation that people COULD fill my every need. This is not to say that the meals, the texts, the childcare, the kind souls who shoveled my snow, the truest friends who would drop everything so I could go to the doctor or get free time were not noticed and appreciated. They were. So needed and so noticed. But it is to say that for the spouse whose husband or loved one is deployed (for anyone), there is truly nothing that can fill your soul completely other than God. No act of love from any person can replace the true satisfaction God can provide. For me, it took removing the ability of being able to rely on people for me to see how I could only rely on God.

People can carry me, walk with me, love me, encourage me, and point me to the one who can sustain me. That sustaining can only come from God.

I am never thirsty and fully satisfied as I drink deeply of the well of Jesus, surrounded by others desperately loving Jesus with all they have and loving me (imperfectly, but loving me still) at the same time.

NINE

INTERVIEW FOUR: THERE IS SO MUCH RICHNESS

This friend is one who offered me much hope in her interview. She reminded me to delve into the struggles because that is where our true hearts are revealed and shaped and changed. She wasn't afraid to share honestly because she has seen God work in her sharing. She is welcoming, warm, and wise. Enjoy and soak up her words.

ANNA: What has military life been like for you?

FRIEND: I don't know how I could do it without faith. I am involved with a women's ministry that is an extension of the Protestant service. Every military installation has a PWOC, or Protestant Women of the Chapel. I have been involved in it, heavily in Alaska and then in Georgia and now. PWOC is where I have poured into ministry the most. I have been a retreat speaker. I have been involved in the FRG, or Family Readiness Group. I have been the treasurer twice and then a key caller and a participant but never the leader or director. I did a lot in Alaska right when we got there, and we were heavily involved in the FRG. We would meet every month. That was a great way to jump into military life.

Most of what I've learned is from failure or from someone else who has done it. I can't claim I did all this really well or that it was done with a joyful heart.

A story to share is that because of COVID, my husband and his unit did not have a welcome home party or anything like that. They just said pick them up here and so I went at 2 a.m. and he hopped in the car. My parents brought the kids over in the morning. I filmed from behind the kids and when my daughter saw my husband, she said: "Mommy really struggled while you were away. Daddy, I really miss you." It was very humbling. I still have it on camera.

ANNA: How long have you been in the military and how many stations?

FRIEND: We have been in for six years and we have been at four stations. He went to Fort Jackson and then to Fort Benning. I lived in Texas and my daughter was born in March and he was at Fort Benning. My husband was not there for my daughter's birth. I moved back and forth between my parents' house and our assignments. When my daughter was born, I was induced on Friday and then he met her on Saturday morning.

I moved in with my in-laws during COVID. My pride stole a lot from me because I wanted to do a lot by myself. Don't let your pride steal from you. Be willing to state your needs. Be willing to ask for help because I didn't.

I hit my breaking point before I asked for help. I had a "battle buddy"—we met through PWOC. She has a degree in counseling. After a long time of me struggling, she said: "I am going to ask: What do you need right now?" I finally said: "I just need to work out." We figured out that is a tangible need—we can find a way to do that. Find out one thing you do to thrive and solve that problem. Think about your tangible needs and find a way to meet them.

Instead of me stewing and saying, "Why are they not helping me with this?", I needed to realize I wasn't asking people to help. It's not fair to them. Have humility and ask for help. It's okay.

ANNA: What helped you prepare pre-deployment with kids and your family?

FRIEND: We made the daddy dolls. Because of their ages, I didn't tell them until less than a week before. We did family things; we went to the zoo. For my husband, I wrote pictures and cards and letters and scriptures.

We had to take care of things logistically on the front end for me—finances, bills, power of attorney, communicating expectations. Do these things, so that you can support him well. Make sure to have one-on-one time with your husband before he goes.

For me, I want to share my personal story with Jesus. My prayer going into this last deployment was: "Lord, I want to be closer to you than ever before and I want my marriage to be stronger after this than it was before." When my husband left, I thought we were at the best place. Then, we saw each other for a brief time when I could meet up with him and I realized: We have a lot to work on. In some ways, it was good not being in the same house and in the same bed because I could process with the Lord and then communicate with my husband about it. I was able to work on my issues on my own and share with him what I was learning.

I was reading a book called *Every Bitter Thing Is Sweet* and the author talks about relating to the Lord with her emotions. I started realizing that I don't engage with my emotions well. There is a piece with the Lord that I am missing out on and so I want to spend time this year doing that. People say that the Psalms are a way to engage with your emotions, so I started reading that. Someone recommended a book called *How We Love*. It talks about love and attachment styles and that brokenness in childhood can be carried into marriage. Some of it is learning to heal from childhood and how we have carried hurts into marriage. Both of us had done damage to one another and we had to see that.

ANNA: What helped you during deployment?

FRIEND: Realize your capacity will be diminished and it is okay to say no to things or not to sign up for things.

Don't wait to do the things you want to do. Pour into your community and church community. There isn't a need to protect family time like you normally might when your whole family is together so you can get to know others in a different way.

In supporting my husband, we would send pictures, stories, letters, and packages. We tried to send love above and beyond. We did try to protect the time he was available, as in if he was calling, we would stop what was going on to focus on him. I found that if he called, the call would get derailed by the kids. So, we would plan once a week to have time on the phone that was after the kids went to bed or when they were still in bed, so we could talk one on one. We had the chance to see each other in the middle of the deployment and during this time we built on good communication and transparency.

I would sometimes run to mentors first rather than my husband, but I learned my husband needs to be the first person. We read books together and talked about the books—this allows you to do something together while being separate and it gives you something to talk about aside from the kids or what he is doing or what you are doing. I also think having community and having "a battle buddy," or someone you can share honestly with and pray with, is necessary.

Weekends can be really hard. It should be a respite but it's not. We found that having someone that can do things with you and be with you helped so much. Our "battle buddy" came over for dinner and helped me put the kids to bed.

Having trips or things to look forward to helps. That is what feeds my soul: experiences. I would try to bring other people along on those experiences.

Even though my husband was not here, I went to visit his family. Even though you may not want to, including his family in your plans helps them feel connected even with him gone.

I also suggest having good rhythms. We put our kids in a Mother's Day Out. It gave me two days a week where the bigger kids were gone. I also embraced this mentality: On Thursday, I needed to plan nothing. I need to rest and just be with the Lord. Pick a day to just be.

As far as helping the kids during deployment, I would say: Speak highly of the Army (or your military branch) and speak highly of what Dad is doing. You want it so that kids say what Dad is doing is good. Or, say: "Isn't it cool that God is using him and he has a job?" Explain to your kids what he is doing and that he is in a different place and that he is working hard. Deployment is hard but what he is doing is a good and noble thing. Explain that it is just for a season and you can't give them an end date.

We would keep a list of the things we wanted to do when daddy got home. For example, when daddy gets home, let's get this kind of party—a pizza party. When daddy gets home, it is going to be the best.

Because of COVID, we had to quarantine. We couldn't go anywhere, couldn't see any other family, and this actually allowed us to have memorable family time when he got back with just us.

ANNA: What advice would you give to someone facing a first deployment?

FRIEND: Don't view it as a time that is wasted. There is such richness and growth. There is more time and space to do things you don't normally do. I drove to Kentucky twice and flew once to visit a mentor. Don't say, "That's too hard," or that you can't do something or that you can't find someone that can help you. Because your loved one is gone, you can actually have a unique time to do things you normally wouldn't. I read through the Bible chronologically and saw the richness of digging into God's Word daily.

I remember when my daughter was born and my husband was gone often. I would put her to bed and sing "Lord I Need You" and I would pray. I knew I couldn't even pretend that I didn't need God. My daughter saw me in those moments. I would rather my daughter see me struggle and run to Jesus rather than just seeing me say: "I'm fine, everything's fine." Being fine is impossible, but her seeing my imperfections makes Jesus more beautiful to her. That's humbling but that's what I really want. My flesh cringes but it's good. In innocence or ignorance, I want to pray for those things. My husband and I are closer today and I am more like Jesus today. There is so much more richness. Because of COVID, my husband's deployment was extended. Instead of being bitter, I decided to use that time to take another trip to see a friend. I want to see the richness in God's provision.

ANNA: How did you handle the season of postdeployment or reentry into the home?

FRIEND: Protect reintegration time. Quarantine was a good excuse to say no—"This is for us"—and creating that time for him and I to reintegrate well. We wanted to be just slow and still. We went on a family walk every night and that was it. Communicate expectations before he comes home. I have a friend who has done six deployments and it still can be hard.

I know from others who have done deployments before that they have certain advice such as: Communicate expectations ahead of time. You might say: "Before, we did this, can we try these different things now?" You might say: "These are hopes I have. These are fears I have." Think about those things ahead of time.

It's hard because you might have said: "You want to change these things, but I want to see you change in this area." The other person might say: "I will fail you." Plan out what to say when those fears are real and communicate that. We had those conversations beforehand.

Coming back to when my daughter said: "Mommy really struggled while you were away"—my daughter saying that makes me feel like I wasn't a good wife or mom. I had to come back to a place of realizing I was acting like I had it all together. I started acting really erratic and getting really spun up. I had to tell my husband: "I am confessing to you that I want your approval more than the approval of God. The Lord has walked with me through the last year. He knows and He is with me. I want Him to be glorified." I had to realize that ultimately what the Lord thinks of me is what matters. My husband and I had to learn to communicate authentically—to share our true and honest feelings and work through those together.

I had to pray a lot. Because I was learning to engage with the Lord and with my emotions, this took a lot out of me. I was trying to be raw with the Lord. But He meets us in our fears. It was constant and raw when I finally began to explore my feelings with the Lord and with myself.

I learned to be gracious during postdeployment. One thing I did was saying "my kids," so I had to learn to say "our kids." Because I had learned to function separately, I had to remind myself—these are his kids too!

Asking questions like: "How can I best love you right now?" You have probably heard of the love languages test but your love languages may have drastically changed. So retaking it and applying it currently can be helpful. I recharge by being alone or going on a run. My husband was very good to say "Go!" and let me go and run guilt free. Letting him parent was a huge adjustment when he came back. He is the head of the household and we had to remember and embrace that. For me, giving my husband alone time with each of the kids was important and just, in general, creating time for family. Wanting him to have one-on-one time with his family is good and prioritizing that is good.

ANNA: What were some of your best moments during deployment?

FRIEND: Growth. Personal growth. The uniqueness of having time with God. I went on some awesome trips—I went to Poland and saw him. I went on some adventures. During COVID, we moved in with his family and we had unique time for the kids to get to know their grandparents.

ANNA: What were some of your hardest moments during deployment?

FRIEND: To note: They were all caused by pride. I now have the tools to be able to choose to walk in humility instead of walking in pride. But, during that time, I didn't even see it. I would say: "I'm doing great, I'm doing great," but I was trying to do it all myself. I need help from people. I had a breakdown in November when I was asking: "Why are people not meeting my needs?" and then other people were saying: "You aren't communicating your needs!" Because I told people "I'm fine," sometimes I would reject family. COVID allowed me to move in with family but I will say this: You aren't meant to do it on your own. Taking on the hard is meant for God and not for you.

I remember it was on Easter Sunday and I was trying to process childhood wounds. But I wasn't authentic with the people I was around. I didn't realize it takes a lot of emotional energy to do that and I was in a volatile place and I didn't want to bring people in. I could have said: "Hey, could you give me an hour or two to have by myself?" But I didn't say that. I moved into his parent's house and it amplified the fact that he was gone. I would say: "I have to leave and I need some space." At one point, I took two days and moved back to my own house. I would go during the day and then come home at night. I needed time to recharge by myself.

The hardest moments were when I let my pride steal from me. But I learned the gift of confession. I chunked it on a shelf and was like "I don't know what this is" but to take it out and say: "I am going to confess this and bring it into the light, and it won't have that power anymore." The minute I see pride or control then I can confess it. But if I hadn't gone through this deployment, I wouldn't know that. A deeper level of authenticity and the ability to process emotions and own my weakness brought me to a beautiful place. At one point, I even said: "I didn't know marriage could be this rich."

ANNA: Do you have any advice for how to accept help?

FRIEND: Ask yourself the question: "What do I need right now?" or ask your battle buddy: "Is this selfish of me?" and understand that your capacity is diminished. Wherever your capacity is, it is diminished. I think it is important to learn to communicate with someone else instead of saying: "I'm fine" or "I don't need someone else."

I cannot stress enough the importance of being tied to a church community. Sometimes, our kids go through different developmental stages. For example, my son was really difficult at one point and our friend at our church said: "I am going to give you one-on-one time with him." Normally, a spouse can do that. Sometimes the kids might need guy time with a brother or father-in-law or someone that can fill that role. The same is true with daughters—there are times that a male can love her in ways that I can't.

ANNA: Are there resources the military offers that you have utilized and enjoyed?

FRIEND: Family Readiness Groups. Go to as many as you can. Don't be jaded by the term *FRG* if you had a bad experience with one in the past. Go into a new one without a bias against it. With most rotations and deployment, they give childcare which is helpful, and I have had friends who have used it.

I also used other resources such as volunteer opportunities and Army community services. I took classes such as Army family team building. They have Army 101 and FRG 101. I live off post here. Embrace wherever you are at. I hurt for people or wives who move to a place and then their husband deploys but then they choose to move home. You miss a lot of things but you also get uninterrupted time with family. But don't run from a really cool opportunity to embrace where you are planted. Don't just wait for them to get back. Take time to still go hiking or still go exploring or enjoy all that the place where you are stationed has to offer. Get plugged into a church or a chapel. We have gone to church off post. Get plugged into your actual neighborhood and get to know the people around you.

ANNA: Anything else you want to add?

FRIEND: I think sometimes military wives can take frustrations out on the military or circumstance, but I would often say: "I can do this all myself." Just being authentic and saying what is true: "This is hard but God is good." We can be frustrated with what we know to be true and we can be wrestling with it. You want me in the raw rather than cowering from God and God wants intimacy with you.

Anyone I spoke to or tried to ask for advice would say: "Have a military mentor and, if you can, have one who is maybe a couple years ahead of you. Someone that is willing to be brutally honest with you and willing to pray with you. Someone who is willing to say, 'Why is this so hard for you?' and you can be pushed beyond a tough place."

The First Deployment

Embrace the uniqueness of deployment and try to view it through the lens of God's sovereignty. Try not to walk in fear, and confess if you do have fear to God and to others.

End of Interview

This friend was sincere, forthright, and unbarred. She didn't shy away from sharing the embarrassment of hearing her daughter say she was struggling or sharing what it was like to encounter her pride. Her willingness to swing wide open the doors of her soul eased me into doing the same. How could I see the richness in the season of deployment? How could I see it as unique and value its distinctness? How could I flip upside down my view of it and see how it could benefit me and grow me? With this friend's humility, I felt confident that I could take steps to begin the process of viewing deployment through the lens of its richness.

TEN

SWEET PEA

I n high school, I was the girl who put the whoopee cushion on the teacher's chair. I once did fifteen belly flops into the pool because my friends thought it was funny.

"Anna! Anna!" my friends shouted, and then filled with the attention and audacity I needed, I flew belly first into the pool, blood vessels popping as I took the flop full on, then swimming right back up to the ladder to do it again.

At one point in my life, laughing was my highest priority and avoiding anything serious was my goal. This served me well in many ways. And, in many ways, as I realize now, it did not.

While this joke mentality has been my default, it hasn't always helped me process hard and difficult and sad things in my life. It's a blocking mechanism I used to push others away, to send a message that says, "I'm okay and I'm laughing, see? Don't pity me. I've got this. I'm fine. To show you I'm fine, I will make you laugh so you feel better that I'm not sad." It puts joke first and reality second. Because, often, I'm not fine. Sometimes, I'm sad and I'm grieving or I'm angry, and yet I still feel this need to put on a face for the world that I've got it under control. What do we keep in and what do we show others and why?

Many of us develop these blocking mechanisms but they might express themselves in different ways. Maybe we over exercise to cover our sadness or over eat or drink to excess or choose to small talk with our friends instead of talk about the real stuff, the hard stuff. There are a lot of ways we can choose to drown out, ignore, numb, force down, or cover what is really going on.

But, in the end, these blocking mechanisms, they don't work. The feelings are still there, and in a healthy emotional world, we need to find a way to process what's really going on.

One way we can figure out what's really going on with ourselves or others is if there are things that aren't matching in our words and actions or body language. For example, we might laugh while crying because we feel embarrassed. Or, we might say "I don't know why I am crying, I never cry" or "I am not supposed to cry." We pretend to be strong. Or, we might say "I forgive you" but our hands are clenched in a fist and the anger is still there festering. As a counselor, we look for these types of things that are incongruent and, if it's appropriate, we might call them out to our client to help them uncover what's really going on. Sometimes, we can't see these inconsistencies ourselves and we need help (I was obviously in this boat and needing help seeing my joke default).

I remember when we found out I was pregnant with my second child. We had just spent a year raising my first daughter—a year of spit up, pureed food on brightly colored spoons, soft blankets, burp rags, diapers, and snuggles. It was a year of stumbling and learning and a year of bliss. When we started trying for baby number two, we were also trying to plan a pregnancy around the military, so the timing of the pregnancy seemed like it would fit in with Tony's schedule. I had started tracking the size and saw that he or she was the size of a sweet pea. I was already starting to get excited thinking about my first daughter being a big sister. I ordered those pregnancy reveal items to tell the grandparents and aunties and uncles. I was already imagining nursery ideas and wondering if the little one was a boy or a girl. I was planning a trip to see my family and was excited to tell my sister and mom and friends from back home. Don't we always have perfect plans in our mind?

A few days after we found out I was pregnant, I was experiencing symptoms that were concerning and decided to go to the doctor to get checked up. As the doctor did the sonogram, she gently told me there was no heartbeat. Man, two words that I wish no one had to hear. Little sweet pea was only with us for six short weeks.

It's not easy to share. It's hard to even say out loud. It felt wrong, like I was weak, unable, unhealthy. Like my body failed. A little one had died in me. I started thinking about all the things I could have done to cause it and blaming myself. I started wondering who that little sweet pea was and what God's purpose could possibly be in this.

I wanted to say something to fix it. I wanted to be strong. I wanted it to not have happened. I tried to revert back to my joke default and my fake joyful face when I talked about it. Not gonna lie, I've gotten pretty good at this. My sister-in-law called me out. She reminded me that it's okay for it to just hurt and just not be okay. I didn't have to wrap it up in this perfect bow of processing and present it to the world with the Christian answer. I didn't have to say, "It's hard but—." It's okay for it to just be hard.

Sometimes I didn't want to talk about it because it was just easier that way, to not say it out loud, to not have to then engage the topic and thus prick my wounds further. Pushing people away felt easier. Isolation felt easier. Silence felt easier. Talking about anything other than what was actually going on felt easier.

But then, sometimes, I felt like all I wanted to do was talk about it. Remember it. Freeze the world so that this little life wouldn't be forgotten. Make the world stop continuing on because this little life didn't get to continue on and it's not fair. Scream about it. Talk about this little life and who they were and what they would have been like. Were they a boy or a girl? What would he or she have looked like? Sometimes, I couldn't bear the small talk, like the world was talking about all the wrong things.

With the loss of little sweet pea, I'm reminded about the grieving process and that it's okay for it to be hard and for me to know that some days will be worse than others. Feeling sad at unexpected moments is normal and part of the process. I go in and out of sadness and that's okay. Some days it lingers. Little reminders and memories and thoughts take hold and take over.

Things I struggle with:

- Blaming (others and myself),
- Wishing (that this wasn't what God had for me), and
- Trusting (that God is still good in all of this).

I started thinking about the big questions of life and the theology behind life, and the nerd in me wanted answers. I wanted to know what the future holds. I wanted to know what to do next. I wished I could say I had all of the answers figured out. But the truth is I don't and I don't think I ever will.

I can know all the counseling theories and yet my default is really ingrained in me—those inconsistencies and blocking mechanisms. I want to hide the hard, make it better somehow. I continue to want to put on a pretend face that everything is okay. I have to work towards awareness and authenticity every day, asking Jesus to help me be real with myself and others.

After my miscarriage, I held my daughter (who was one at the time) closer, I played longer, I was more patient and more gentle. I laughed a lot at her silliness and cried as I held her. I let her snuggle as long as she wanted. The reality that life truly is short, and the seconds are precious really sunk in.

In all of this, though, here's what I know about the hard moments: I can't trust my feelings to tell me what's true. I have to cling to God's truth. And what I know is that God says even when it feels hopeless, we always have hope. When we feel defeated, God always has a plan for victory. And even in death there is life.

What I also know to be true but does not necessarily feel true is that sharing helps ease the burden. Our tendency can be to isolate—it hurts too much to share the pain because it brings awareness to the pain. Bringing awareness allows others to hold you up, even in the smallest ways. It grants those who care for you the privilege of walking with you and alongside of you in your pain. There is power in saying out loud what you truly feel. There is power in letting others share the load.

I hope that one day I can meet our tiny, sweet pea. But, until then, I am going to entrust my little sweet pea, and all that's in my life right now and all that is in my life in the past, the pain and the worry and the wondering and the scared and all of my future, to the creator of all life, a God who gives me hope in the hard.

ELEVEN

THE BIRTH STORY

Choosing to have kids and try and get pregnant is not a straight and narrow path. It is more like a jagged, switchback hike with a lot of wandering, dawdling, moving between determination and depletion, wondering if the hike was worth it type of path. For some, maybe it wasn't a choice but an accident. For some, it is easy—a couple weeks off birth control and they're pregnant. For others, it is a story of loss and grief, of walking with their partner through ups and downs of infertility and miscarriage and medical procedures. There is loss of control of your body—you can't force it to happen no matter how hard you wish or dream or plead or beg. There is loss of control of your body even in pregnancy—finding out you are pregnant and the jubilation that comes with that knowledge, followed by a fear or worry of losing the pregnancy for some. Add on to all of this the military life—for some, constant moves mean not having the same obstetrician or pediatrician or hospital or not having your imagined nursery or house or time to decorate the way you hoped or not knowing others or having community in the area you are living in. Add on to this the not knowing when or if your partner can be there for any of it or (even if they are) for how long.

The story of sweet pea was written in March of 2018. We found out in October 2018 that I was pregnant again. Pregnancy brought the immediate questioning if the pregnancy would be a miscarriage again. Then, there was military life. I was still holding on to my plan because I remember thinking: *I can do a deployment but I could never have a baby without my husband there.*

We found out in winter 2019 that my husband would likely deploy in May 2019, and my due date was June 25. So, yeah, my plan wasn't looking too good. "A man plans his course but the Lord determines his steps." (Proverbs 16:9)

Denial was my first reaction when I felt the contractions two weeks early. My husband had left three weeks ago, and this was not part of the birth plan. The plan was for him to be there, coaching, pulling my hair back when I threw up, quietly encouraging, handling the details that become fuzzy when pain became all I could process. I had set an induction date so he could be there. These contractions were starting a few days before that date.

When I lose control, I find myself grasping onto anything I can to make sense of the loss. Even while experiencing contractions, I was thinking: *Maybe it's just false labor pains.* Even when my sister-in-law came over to check on me and suggested we go to the hospital just to get checked up, I thought: *Maybe it's just false labor pains.* When we got to the hospital, I didn't even know what to pray. Do I pray for Tony to be here? Do I pray for the pains to go away? Deep breaths, one step, then another. My sister-in-law took on the role of distraction: playing music that made us dance, laughing at the sounds of moans in rooms around us (what else can you do?). She brought the game Splendor and had to explain the game instructions at least five times and basically played the game with herself as I sat in a hospital gown, back open, wincing every now and then, unsure what to expect, half-attempting to play because distraction did feel good.

Eventually, the labor pains seemed to taper off. This was part of the plan it seemed. Or, did I even have a plan? I tried to release control but at the same time letting go completely felt undoable. The medical team stated we could check out. I thought: *This is perfect, my husband can come later next week.* I tried to spend the rest of the day doing normal, everyday things we loved to do. I took Jemma to the park, trying to trust that if I took each step one at a time, the steps I needed to take would reveal themselves, still unsure of the future. I found myself at one point at the park, bending over in a porta-potty to help my toddler pull up her pants and had to hold the wall of the porta-potty to steady myself. I felt weak and nauseous. Probably, I had felt like this all day, but I wasn't ready to face it. We drove to McDonald's for a Happy Meal for Jemma. When I couldn't even drive without feeling like I needed to pull over because of the pain, I knew I needed to text my in-laws. Back to the hospital we went.

My sister-in-law held my hand as I doubled over in pain. She prayed for me. She cried with me in the hardest pains. She made me laugh like only she can. She reminded me God was in control. She called our team "the girl squad" and a group of lady nurses came around me. When it was explained to the team that my husband was deployed, there was a feeling of nurturing, empowerment, bonding. My obstetrician even came in on her normal night off to help with my birth. My other sister-in-law came in and helped us all remain calm and steady. Eileen (Eila) Grace was born on June 10.

I remember the night she was born, and my sister-in-laws slept in the hospital bed next to me. I got very little sleep, waking up to Eila's every little stir and whimper. But I remember just wanting to take in every moment of God and His provision. To taste it and hold it, to bask in the light of knowing God had been there all along. It didn't matter that Tony hadn't been there. It didn't matter that Eila had been born at a time I would not have planned for or that even in my exhaustion I still wasn't sleeping. What mattered was God had shown me His love in the details. The details of her tiniest toes and sneezes. All of her little five-pound self. I remember thinking about the miscarriage and how it felt to give over my worry and anxiety about Eila's life to Him. To trust that every breath she gets is one given to her by the Lord of the universe.

That trust takes work. It is a moment by moment, worry by worry, thought by thought trust. It feels like all gained can be lost and then it feels like all can be steady, peace, wave after wave. I feel like I can both trust myself to trust and I absolutely cannot trust myself to trust. But when I think about that hospital night— just basking in a complete visual of God's goodness, I could trust. Eila, a little five-pound reminder. Eila, grief from loss turned into celebration of life. Five pounds of not wondering but seeing in the flesh how God can provide even when two people who love each other are separated by oceans and countries, how God can provide when even the smallest life didn't get to live in you.

I believe God gives us these graces to have as visual memories. "Remember", God says. "Remember these moments." And I can come back to these moments to see His grace.

Month after month as Eila grew, I felt like even in her screams I would remind myself of how life is a gift. I allowed myself to think about sweet pea and the life that didn't get to live and this made me embrace the screams. Screams meant life. Thankfulness gives perspective. It is a balm for grief. It brings hope for the future.

We can plan and plan and fret and worry and overanalyze and worry again, but God provides. He has a plan. Trust Him to carry your hardest burdens. If it had been my plan, Tony would have been there for labor and delivery. In my plan, I never would have gotten to experience seeing my sister-in-laws love me so well during Eila's birth. In the labor pains, in the missing of the moment when my baby could have met her dad, in the intense chasm of emotion, in it all, I felt closer to God in those moments than the easy ones. Working my plan would mean taking out the true depth of knowing God in that way. My Lord and my God is the one I spoke to through it all. The one who created every fiber of my being, every hair on my head, who knows my thoughts before I even think them. The same Lord who created every tiny fingernail, every little millimeter, every molecule of my Eila. That is the Lord who still holds the baby from my miscarriage. That is the Lord who is in His timing brought life into this world and reminded me of His goodness. It is our souls and hearts that have to believe it, no matter who is physically present with us.

I never thought I could do a birth without Tony. We are all capable of so much more than we realize. God gives us the power and strength in the hardest of hard. He surrounds us with His faithfulness when we have eyes to see it. Thank you, my God and my Jesus. Not for a moment does He leave us. God was faithful through our miscarriage and in the timing of our pregnancy. God was faithful in Eila's birth. God was faithful in Eila's ability to eat well and breastfeed, something Jemma struggled with as a baby and something I had worried about. God was faithful in providing many who have loved our family during the time right after her birth as well as the many months after during deployment in ways I never could have imagined. God is faithful. In whatever you are facing, I promise He is. Dwell on His promises and His truth and watch as they remain true (maybe not in ways you would expect, but they remain true).

TWELVE

INTERVIEW FIVE: THE DARK AGES

T his veteran military spouse helped me analyze my own response to deployment and step back to evaluate how I could be growing and being better myself. When I first texted her about the interview, she said, "I sure don't feel qualified." She is one hundred and million percent qualified. She has lived and breathed the hardest of the hard and shares with grace and depth.

ANNA: How long were you in the military and how many stations were you at?

FRIEND: Twenty-six years, and thirteen moves. There is a saying in the Air Force: "Home is where the Air Force sends you."

ANNA: What helped you prepare pre-deployment with kids and your family?

FRIEND: I didn't tell my kids too much about it because they would get sad. I wouldn't tell the kids a particular date because that always seemed to change. We homeschooled so that helped because we made our schedule. When it came close, we tried to do special events before he left. We tried to keep everything as normal as possible. No one taught me so I had to figure out for myself what to do and what was best.

ANNA: What helped during deployment?

FRIEND: I tried to keep a normal routine as much as possible. We kept a mentality of "we are going to keep going on like we have before." I homeschooled so there was comfort in that they always had me available. When we were in Germany, Friday nights we would go to a swimming pool, eat pizza, and then come home and watch a movie. On Saturdays, I joined other wives and played bingo and then they had a gigantic room for the kids to run around. It was on a regular basis and it was good to hang around other wives—we got a lot of fellowship that way. I got into a regular Bible study that way and that was when I first became a Christian. We would have our boys eat together and then let our kids be in the nursery while we went to the Bible study. I did let my kids sleep in my bed during deployment and it was special that they could sleep in my bed. We would wake up and be tickling on Saturday mornings. So, we would do some things the same but not all things the same.

I remember once we had just moved from an Air Force to an Army base. I didn't understand the acronyms and didn't understand his job. Also, it was wartime. My parents had a guesthouse in Hawaii and offered for me to come stay with them. But I felt called to stay on the base that my husband had deployed out of. It was Desert Storm and that is where he would have been sent back if he were injured, so I felt like I needed to be there.

Back then, it was kind of like "The Dark Ages" with FaceTime or Skype—less ability to communicate but now there are so many options. Even my son and daughter-in-law dated through deployment and decided to get married and were able to use those communication methods to date effectively.

During Desert Storm, they would give us ten minutes on the phone. The person would say: "Your ten minutes is up" and you would have to hang up—it didn't matter where you were in the conversation. It was harder to connect because you didn't want to tell them problems because you just wanted to hear that they were fine. Talking to him felt like a brownie that you want and can smell it but you can't have it. He would call at weird hours. I would send letters and not know if he got them, but I would hope he got them. Everything after that deployment felt like a piece of cake.

ANNA: What advice would you give to someone facing a first deployment?

FRIEND: Don't stuff feelings. It's okay to have feelings and be angry or sad. Talk about your feelings. Talk about them with your husband and talk about them with friends. Have a support group—whether it is coworkers or church—just have a support group. Don't isolate yourself. It will make it harder to be isolated. You can feel overwhelmed or depressed, but you can't totally give into those feelings. You might have bad days and turn down things you might normally do, but don't isolate for long periods of time. I tried to make a goal while he was gone—to try something new, such as running or badminton or knitting. I once made the goal of completing a triathlon and I did it!

What happens about six weeks before is that there is a lot of tension, knowing your loved one is going to go. I warned someone once and they said: "I'm glad you told me"—it truly does happen! You will get in a fight about something small but it's the nerves, the anticipation, and the edge. It will be stupid and you will laugh about it later. You might be thinking: "He's kind of a jerk right now." I always kind of felt like: "A little break would be nice." We would get upset with each other and I came to get used to it—the tension happens. I didn't stress over it and it happened. He will come back and you'll say, "I did love you!"

ANNA: How did you handle the season of postdeployment or reentry into the home?

FRIEND: That is one reason why we kept a routine so that when he comes back, it's the same. I would remind him: "It's the same." While they are gone, you might take on extra roles. I took over finances because we kept it the same. You have to remind husbands and fathers: "This is the way we've done it." When they get back, don't change the routine and try to say: "Let's not do big changes right now." The guys like to dive right back in. Dad has to discipline the way you have been disciplining. The wives have accomplished so much and it can be hard if things change. Try to do a little "honeymoon" away when your loved one comes back. We would wait awhile and possibly get away a couple months later, because the kids really wanted time with their dad.

ANNA: What were your best moments during deployment?

FRIEND: I would learn new things—like I learned to knit. I got a wives group going in Alaska and we would try to do something Alaskan. We would try snowshoeing or cross-country skiing—that was really fun. When my husband was in Germany, I learned to make apple strudel—that is a fun memory. I tried new things often during deployment and I didn't have to worry about if my husband would have liked the activity—I just did it. In Germany, we would try some of the different restaurants and would order new food we hadn't tried before. In England, we did some fun shopping trips. We tried to immerse ourselves in the culture as much as we could.

ANNA: What were your hardest moments during deployment?

FRIEND: The hardest moments were definitely during Desert Storm when my husband was at war. I could not really communicate except through letters, and I did not ever know what was happening. I only got German television so I couldn't listen to American news. I didn't have the Internet. I would have to drive on post and I could get a little bit of news but I didn't want a lot because I didn't want to dwell on it. I had a six-year-old, a three-year-old, and a newborn. Just not knowing was so hard.

The First Deployment

When we were in England, on television people were speaking English so I could at least know what was going on, but we couldn't communicate during that either. I had to have patience. When we were in England, the jets deployed to Korea and we basically had 24 hours' notice before he had to leave. You would kiss them goodbye and not know what would happen.

ANNA: Do you have any advice for how to accept help?

FRIEND: Remember: It's not a big deal to ask for help. I tell everyone you can't be an expert in everything. We are all better at some things than other things. We can't do it all and do it all well. Ask for help. I think we all love to help others and would be happy to help others. Someday, someone around you will need help and we help those we love. We love getting to help those we love. So, get over yourself and ask for help.

I remember during Desert Storm—my car broke down and we had a house fire. The very first Sunday my husband left and then my car broke down and I had three kids in the car. I had to call my husband's first sergeant and he towed it. I remember the tow chain broke and smashed the windshield. Then, even with all of that, the toilet downstairs clogged up and it was during Christmas. The toilet was clogged with poop and no one fixed it for a week because, in that country, they didn't have handymen coming out during that time—and I had to just tape it closed. In the midst of that hard time, I had just become a Christian. It was just trying to trust that all this stuff doesn't really matter and it will get fixed. Most people want to help other people. Just remember that. Everyone gets it in the military. I normally say I would love to help watch kids or help someone. Let someone do something for you.

ANNA: Was there anything I missed that you would like to share?

FRIEND: There is a book I loved: *Be Safe, Love Mom.* She has four kids and all four kids are all in different military services. Her kids are constantly deploying. She took a job to teach in another country just to understand what it was like over there.

I have a funny memory of Desert Storm in that I rarely got a phone call. I remember I got a phone call once but the phone was downstairs and I was running down the stairs thinking it was my husband calling for an update and I broke my toe trying to get to the phone in time, but it turns out it was my mother-in-law. She was on the East Coast and could never do the math about what the time difference was.

End of Interview

This friend made me pause and consider the past plight of those who support the military and their loved ones who were in many kinds of war situations. I was ashamed at how tempted I had been to complain about my own deployment experience when I took time to consider her troubles. How has technology advanced, aiding our communication with our loved ones currently? But also: How could we, present women supporting those we love in the military, relate to the women of the past? No matter the advancement of technology and communication, couldn't we all relate to our prayer for the safety of our loved ones, our journey of handling the stresses of support from home, our own failures in doing so and learning along the way? We are linked—the present and the past—and we are launched in strength forward, carrying their pain and carrying their power.

THIRTEEN

HELP

I t's not an easy topic. Help. How do we accept it humbly? How do we give it in a way that truly does help? I think about it often. As a person who has given help poorly and has received help poorly and basically just failed at help all around, I know there has to be a better way. Or, at least I want to try for one.

I didn't know how to ask for help or how to think about help in the right way during the deployment. But then I started asking: How do I help others? How do I act when I am the one helping? As I think about how I most needed help in deployment, it also spurred me to evaluate how I give help. This chapter might be a good one to share with others who want to help during deployment and also a good one to think about how we ourselves give help.

1. Sometimes, I've wanted to help others in my life; not because I truly wanted to, but because I felt guilty that I felt I had to. Isn't that a selfish desire to help? Isn't that in fact a desire to help myself be seen as a helper, not a desire to actually help someone? But if I'm being honest, I want others to help me out of a genuine love for me not because they feel they have to. I think we should all do each other that same service. I think we should say no to helping others

out of guilt. It is exhausting to live a life in the prison of wanting others to see our help, of wanting others to recognize our help, instead of just simply helping because we truly want to help.

2. We should say no to busying our lives so much that we don't have time to stop and help others. But we should also realize that help takes sacrifice and is never comfortable or easy.

3. I once had someone I knew who I would see at a weekly function who would say every week: "I want to have you and Tony over for dinner soon." This happened every single week. It bothered me because this person never, ever followed through with an actual "Let's meet Wednesday at 6 p.m., does that work for you?" It was always "soon." Possible translation: when life gets less busy, when you actually become someone I can make time for or maybe this person just didn't have the social awareness to remember they invited us to dinner seventeen times with no follow through. Every interaction has a responsibility on my end. I could have said, "Hey, how about Wednesday?" and set a time myself. But the point is the offer of kindness wasn't followed through with which leads me to number four.

4. I think it's important to others to commit to an act of kindness. Don't offer if you don't mean it. Maybe don't over commit to a million volunteer things. Maybe find what you are really wanting to give to or are passionate about and commit fully to those. Maybe make more margin in your life to have time to actually have people over or bring a meal to someone or whatever it might be. I'm saying this because I have overcommitted. I have been the worst helper to people I've cared about. I want to be better. I think words matter. Don't say to someone: "I wonder if this would help

you . . . ?" Ask them: "Would this help you?" and then follow through.

5. Helping others according to how they really need help. When Tony has been gone for the military, at times, it is sometimes hard for me to figure out how help is best needed. But when I can communicate it, it's helpful when others can hear and see what I need most and help meet that need. Sometimes all we can do is help others in the best way we can (meal, time, childcare). Evaluate how you can help someone and do that. Sometimes doing something (anything) to show you care is better than doing nothing. Even if someone didn't help me in a way that maybe I felt best helped, it still felt good to know someone cared. I don't think we should be spending our time during deployment or any other time putting a judgment stamp on other's help: this was the "right" way to help; this was the "wrong" way. A good approach is to be at peace with ourselves and thankful for those God brings in our lives to help while they can. If they ask, tell them what might help better in the future. But, if someone helps and tries to be thoughtful, notice the intention.

6. I think it also comes down to this: be willing to do the hard things for people. When I was visiting my sister in Texas, a stomach bug hit us all. Jemma was barfing, Eila was crying, and I was down for the count. My sister and her husband didn't just stand by. They literally cleaned up bits of vomit for me and held the baby, so I could rest when the waves of nauseousness came over me. I needed people to help in ways I didn't even have the energy to communicate so many times on this deployment. I think true help comes down to getting your hands dirty, literally. Washing someone's dishes, cleaning their toilet, raking their leaves,

changing a poopy diaper. Those are the things I didn't have the guts to ask for and the things that sometimes would have truly helped.

7. If true help comes down to getting your hands dirty, then accepting help comes down to allowing others to get their hands dirty for you. I think there is a level of embarrassment, of pride, that gets in the way of accepting and asking for true help. I wish I would have let this go on deployment and asked for what I truly needed. Let go of the fact that you have urine caked on your toilet from seven months ago and ask for help cleaning the toilets. Let go of the fact that you smell like a dumpster and ask for someone to watch your babies so you can take a shower. This is the only way you will feel truly helped, seen, and loved—when you let go of your embarrassment about what you truly need help with and allow others to meet you in that need, whatever that disgusting, can't even talk about it, need might be.

8. I have also learned to try to give others grace. Knowing that I am not perfect, knowing that I have not helped others in the best way, knowing that I have made comments about how I wanted to help but didn't follow through to others, this knowledge has given me the ability to let go of my frustration when people let me down or don't follow through. I know I am not perfect, and I have not followed through at times too.

Here's what helped me most during deployment:

- Friends who hung out with me just doing our normal life, who helped me with putting our babies to sleep, making dinner, the normal, boring stuff—sometimes it was just the mundane things I wanted the most help with, the daily routine things that no one else was there for

- Friends who looked me in the eyeballs and said, "How are you?" and, then, actually listened
- Friends who offered to help and then followed through on what I said I needed help with, saying: "How's Wednesday for a meal? How is next Thursday for me to watch your babies?"
- Friends who pointed me to God's truth when I felt lonely and lost

Help is hard. Hard to figure out how to give help to someone sometimes and hard to accept. But I want to be better. Better at accepting it in humility instead of saying "No, I've got this" and better at being fully committed to giving it to someone. I pray God gives me grace in seeing how to do both. Yes, I'll fail at it. But I truly desire that I can learn how to both give and take help in a way that honors God.

As someone going through a deployment, maybe ask yourself this:

- What would actually help me right now? (An hour of child-care to work out? Someone cleaning the house? Company after the kids go to bed?)
- Have I communicated those needs to those around me?
- If not, what is stopping me?

FOURTEEN

THE MELTING PLACE

A strange paradox emerged for me during deployment: the giving, giving, giving, and the both finding and losing yourself in the giving. There is a melting place between sacrifice and the finding of self. In that place, I wouldn't want to go back to the version of myself I was before. Because the giving molded me and transformed me—the flames and the heat of the deployment forged a stronger metal, built by the hammering knowledge of what I had seen myself do and what I had been through.

As a selfish person, I want to share my version of the story often. I had a gut check often during deployment when I would stop and realize: Tony is struggling too. I focus on myself often because it formed that melting place and that melting place felt like all I could know, but stepping outside of my own fight was needed. Sometimes, it would just be a small comment, a background in the screen of FaceTime. Sometimes, it would be the pictures of our family he draped across the bleak room and locker he was given. Little nuances, nudges that brought me out of my own narrative and into his.

Just last winter, my husband took Jemma, my oldest daughter, out to learn how to ski for the first time. I had committed that night to an interview for this book. There was an ache and a sadness: *I couldn't miss this moment for her.* Then, I realized how that feeling must be the tiniest twinge of what Tony must have felt during deployment. That tiny twinge multiplied by a million and one missed milestones that his heart jolted at not being present for.

I am so unbelievably proud of my guy and our soldiers. Our soldiers give up family time and "normal life" and holidays. Some of them live in a strange place, with a different language and culture, a good thing to experience but also a daily struggle at times. They do their best to push forward together, building friendships with each other, remembering home with wistfulness. They give hours, months, and days of their energy, their determination, their work, their passion—they give it all. They give time away from people they love. Some soldiers give their lives. And for what?

Because they all believe in the value of serving others, of giving the best life to others even at the cost of their own.

I am proud to live in a country where freedom is important and valued and gained even with sacrifice. I will be honest: some days, the melting place, the actual me sacrificing, felt like acute, excruciating agony. It felt like the job took the best of him and we got the leftovers. Some days it was heartbreaking to me that all Jemma had was a screen to talk to her dad. But I am proud. Tony would remind me that they were helping families where he was— this comforted me at times because I imagined a mom like myself, tucking her babies into bed halfway across the world, wishing for their safety and security. This mom deserves peace in her country and peace in her home.

"If a man hasn't discovered something that he will die for, he isn't fit to live." (Martin Luther King, Jr)

FIFTEEN

CREATIVE LOVE

Relationships, like rowing, are the art of working together to go in the same direction, of agreeing to go in the same direction. The cadence, the pace, is set as you both sync, the dip of the oar in the water, the rhythm catching as you communicate. It takes work, it takes practice, it takes knowing each other's strengths and weaknesses.

The day my husband got back from deployment, my three-year-old daughter held his face, studying him, remembering him all over again. COVID had just started to come over to the United States and, unlike a normal welcoming home ceremony, we just picked him up straight from the airport. We spent the evening eating pizza from our favorite place and watching a movie, snuggling as a family. I thought later about this and how different this may have been from other ceremonies—our welcome back ceremony was pizza and a movie. Two weeks prior, he had to quarantine before being able to come back home. We weren't able to send him care packages because the time he was going to be there was too short. FaceTime could be a hit or miss when he was overseas—our time zones were off or we would miss each other because we were busy and not able to talk fully.

Deployment brings the opportunity to love your significant other in creative ways, and military life in general is constantly challenging me to be innovative in how I care for Tony. Overcoming those challenges or obstacles help you to see how your love can fight for one another across oceans and lands. It can feel like obstacle after obstacle can get in the way of your relationship and this can feel defeating. But it also brings growth, change, and flexibility. Love is a commitment—not based on feelings but based on a vow to love each other through changes. It takes work and deployment multiplies that work. But, just as a plant needs to be pruned, the dead things cut off so more growth can happen, so change brings life, new breath, in your relationship.

One of the best questions I started asking was: How can I creatively love Tony? I just started to accept that our relationship would look and feel different during deployment. I tried different ways to show him love even when I felt tired and even when it felt unusual and new or uncomfortable.

My husband and I would set up "date nights" on FaceTime and I would try to make sure the kids were in bed so I could talk then. We read a book together on our own time and then talked about it together. This gave us something to talk about, other than kids or jobs, and to have a fun topic to talk about, something we were both wanting to share about—what we liked or didn't like, what we thought the characters would do, the setting, the next book in the series, etc.

Here are some other ways we worked on our relationship being apart:

- Listening to a podcast and then talking about it. After you listen, think of some questions you can ask each other. Share some themes or phrases that stood out to you.
- Sending care packages. With a newborn and a toddler, it was so hard to find time to do this but I tried to work it

into things we were already doing, such as my kids drawing a picture or putting stickers on a paper and sending it. For me, dropping off the package at the post office felt like the worst errand (car seats, loading up, waiting in a long line, back in the car for car seats), so maybe try to plan to do this when you have a sitter or have prepared time in advance.

- Writing letters to each other. We did this when we were dating and it was fun to activate this form of loving each other. In the letters, we would talk about memories, things that we are struggling with, things we are excited about. We would compliment things we loved about each other. We tried to focus on the positives and end the letter with questions, so we could keep going by answering that question in the next letter.
- Calls for just us. I tried to call him when the kids weren't around because, if they were, they would want to talk to him the whole time. So, I tried not to talk about anything I was really struggling with or set my expectations that it would be a super productive talk when the kids were talking to him too.
- Sharing honestly during talks when I did get time alone to talk with him. For me, it helped me feel like our relationship still had depth and authenticity. I needed to be able to talk to him when I was down, or had questions, or felt like crying. Even if he couldn't answer, I still texted him when I was upset because I needed him to know where I was at, and I wanted our relationship to have that sincerity and not to feel like we had to protect our feelings from each other.
- Marco Polo. We used Marco Polo as a way to stay connected because even with different time zones, you can leave

a message (a recorded video) for each other when you can and he can do the same. It can be frustrating to try and connect and keep missing each other and this app allows you to be able connect even when your times of connecting are limited.

I found that being creative in the way we loved each other strengthened our love. When we see how our relationship can endure this, we can see how true and powerful our love can be. I have found that deployment helps me to feel more thankful for the time with Tony than I would have without the deployment. I look at him truly—noticing the things I fell in love with, the little quirks and characteristics, taking them in. Relationships, like rowing, are work. There is the heart pumping, sweating, gasping for breath, listening, and adapting. Within the work, you can look around and see the beauty—how far you've come from the shore, the sun shining, shimmering on the water, that feeling of pride, of production, of knowing you are working towards something that is good and worthy to work towards with every push forward.

SIXTEEN

INTERVIEW SIX: JUST FLOAT

T his friend's interview left me feeling at peace. Her ability to be fearlessly candid eased my own insecurities and
doubts. She reminded me how God can use even our
darkest thoughts and emotions and how God can use and redeem
the time of deployment, in our lives as the supporter and in the
lives of our families.

ANNA: How long have you been in the military and how many
stations?

FRIEND: My husband joined in 2011. We met in 2013 and married in 2014. We are at our second duty station with a TDY, or
temporary duty travel, for a few months between duty stations.

ANNA: What helped you prepare predeployment with kids
and your family?

FRIEND: We don't allow guests a week prior to the deployment or the week upon return. Spending intentional time alone
as a family and setting aside time with my husband to ask specific questions was important. With kids, one thing I ask before
a deployment is: "What does he want to have input on?" That
way, I'm not taking everything to him but can honor him by taking things to him that he really cares about. During one deployment, he wanted to know about the babysitters we chose. Another

deployment, he wanted input on big school decisions. He also likes being a sounding board for discipline conversations, but gives me the freedom to make decisions on the ground and not have to run them by him. Having a file folder with all the paperwork I could need was helpful and getting a power of attorney so you can do what you need to during deployment.

Three months out from deployment, we look at a calendar. I block weekends and say no to outside commitments. There are things we have to discuss and handle that are heavy and weighty—wills, etc. We ask questions like: How can I best love and serve him during a deployment? We have learned from each of the deployments and can look back and name those things we feel we did well or didn't do well. We ask: How can we do it better next time? This helps us both get the help we need or gives us tools. For example: Right now, during this deployment, I am talking with him about: "Are we going to spank or not going to spank?" Talking with him in advance gives me boundaries so I can move within that field. Sometimes we avoid doing things that would make him feel sad or left out—things we don't do because he would like to be there the first time and experience that with his son.

Once during a deployment, I tried to buy a car and didn't have the right power of attorney. I had to learn this the hard way—that there are certain types and he can approve them all, so knowing to do that in advance would be helpful.

ANNA: What practically helped you during deployment?

FRIEND:

- Marco Polo
- Concrete Conversations—five questions to help with when it feels we don't have anything to talk about—cards you can purchase that give you questions to ask each other
- Date nights if we can schedule it—FaceTiming and planning an activity, reading a book together—when we

could—and talking about it, watching a show—when we could—and talking about it, and participating in church from afar together
- Books about deployment for my infant son
- Recordings of my husband's voice
- Photo books
- Stuffed animals
- My husband sending gifts
- Making it a point to know and understand my husband's job and the people he is with
- Community- having people who can come alongside of you, support you, and listen to you
- Having something to do outside of the home: volunteering, working, etc.
- Remaining active

ANNA: What advice would you give to someone facing a first deployment?

FRIEND:
- Grace upon grace
- Communication. Trust. Talking about something like the enneagram would be helpful.
- We learned from a marriage conference to talk about how we handle stress. When I get stressed, I move inward and won't talk. I am driving hard and show little or no emotion, whereas, he gets emotional when stressed. He might say: "You don't have to be so tough." He would notice that I have my walls up and not sharing much and he might say: "You can tell me what's going on." Underneath a lot of my toughness is stress and sadness and not being able to rely on him in the flesh.

- You're on the same team. Sometimes we can forget this and feel like the other person is the enemy. Remember this simple sentence: You're on the same team!
- Put things on your calendar to look forward to—monthly and quarterly.

ANNA: How did you handle the postdeployment or reentry into the home season?

FRIEND:

- Time together—no guests—no expectations
- Lots of conversations—not expecting him to jump right in with our son. I don't plan things where he will have to be the primary parent until he feels ready.
- Openly discussing changes in community and family commitments
- The military wants them back and makes reintegration hard. You have to be flexible and willing to do the work.

ANNA: My own experience makes me think of the word *bitterness*. Them leaving and them being gone is hard and then as you said: "The military wants them back." Do you get bitter? How do you handle this?

FRIEND: It is so evident and easier to rely on the Lord because your spouse is gone. You can trust God to meet you where you are at. When they are home, you hope they can be present but the Army demands them. I use the words *open hands* and I try to be open-handed with the time right after a deployment. You get bitter because they are home but not able to be present. The dependency you have on God during deployment has to continue on after deployment. Sometimes thinking of military life as an ocean helps. It's such a thrashing back and forth—wave after wave. He could get back for two weeks but not really able to be fully back and then be gone again. It feels like things are beating you down. Instead of fighting the wave, you have to jump in the wave and just float—accept that this is what military life is, trust God to help you through it, just float.

ANNA: What were some of your best moments during deployment?

FRIEND:

- A vacation alone with my son
- Making normal days fun with new things—even just breaking out of the routine
- Getting involved with something I personally love
- Finding someone you trust and using them to babysit regularly, even if you don't have anything planned

ANNA: What were some of your hardest moments during deployment?

FRIEND:

- Big challenges with a child
- Figuring out how to balance everything
- COVID decisions
- Decision fatigue in parenting—leaning on good friends to help with these discussions
- Loneliness

With COVID, parenting decisions can be hard because one week you think an event is fine and then the next week you go to the same event and you don't think it's fine. Making parenting decisions alone is hard. For example, when my son had trouble sleeping, I didn't know what to try. I lean heavily on my friends for those types of decisions. I've just had to learn to find a trusted friend and say: "I'm having a hard time: just tell me what to do, I'm done making decisions," and we talk it through.

Loneliness can be present—especially with COVID. I am an extroverted person but because my person is gone, every level is stunted. I have to put rhythms in place. I have to put plans into my life where I will interact with an adult human.

I had to learn to recognize the change in capacity in deployment and during times of nondeployment. We are all weak. We are all limited. We are all trying to puff ourselves up or find our identity in things other than Christ. Deployment reveals that differently than when your spouse is there.

ANNA: Can you give specific examples of working through your hardest moments with God's truth?

FRIEND: On the last deployment, the hardest moment was when my son was four months old and he wasn't sleeping. It felt like a deep desperation—I remember thinking: *I can't do this. I can't do this.* The big lesson for me was to ask for help and how to acknowledge my limitations. Being in God's Word is so stabilizing—it is life. When it isn't my priority, I feel like I will drown. This deployment I am currently in, the hardest thing has been parenting and how to train up a child and not kill a child. I learned to lean heavily into the people He has provided. The hardest things are those big decisions as a parent. Sometimes, I wanted to do it all and I had to learn to bow out of things.

ANNA: Do you have any advice for how to accept help?

FRIEND:

- Recognize you are limited.
- Recognize you are provided for by a God who knows you and loves you.
- What advice would you give someone else in your situation? Take your own advice.

Line up people ahead of time who you and your spouse feel comfortable with or trust. Make a regular plan for how you will take the help.

I have seen people make excuses for not accepting help, saying "I don't have someone," etc. Planning in advance is helpful. My son goes to school. If they are open, he is at school. On previous deployments, we were at the YMCA every day. Plan time for people to help you. I don't live near our families, but, if you can see a grandparent who wants to do childcare, that helps.

ANNA: I sometimes felt down on myself that my kids weren't getting "the best" or what they needed or deserved. Can you speak to this for myself or other military spouses?

FRIEND:

- God is sovereign and kind and He is the best Dad. When I feel like my son deserves more from his earthly dad, I can point us back to our heavenly Father.
- You're "playing the long game."
- Look to military families who have been doing this a while.

I know it's not right to weigh it on a scale. There can be a lot of anxiety feelings and thoughts: *His dad is gone, he's going to have all these bad things.* I have to remember that God is sovereign and kind. God is with my son and taking care of my son. It is a sweet opportunity to pray for him in that. One of the things a friend said is: "You're playing the long game." Think of it from an eternal perspective. Put it into that perspective. It feels debilitating but it can also be hopeful. I've seen how deployment has grown our marriage. That can happen for a dad and daughters or a dad and sons. I am floored by teenage kids whose dad has been in the military their whole life and they are incredible kids. That really encourages me—the resilience and wisdom of those kids and the reminder of how God can use deployment in the lives of our children.

ANNA: Do you have any advice for getting plugged into new communities?

FRIEND:

- Do it and quickly.
- Be the inviter. Friend the random person on Facebook. If you feel that spark with someone . . . act on it. Then keep acting on it, until they stop responding.

ANNA: Are there any resources you want to share?

FRIEND: One random thing we love for maintaining Daddy/baby or Daddy/small child connection are recordable hearts for a thirty-second message from Daddy from Hallmark. We have one in a stuffed animal and we have another with my husband singing our nighttime songs.

ANNA: Are there any books you love for deployment to read to kids?

FRIEND:

- *Night Catch*
- *My Daddy Is a Hero*
- *Emma the Medevac Pilot* or books like this specific to what the deployed family member does to help explain what they're doing to kids
- *I Love You Near and Far*
- *My Daddy Sleeps Everywhere*
- Recordable storybooks from Hallmark—especially *Under the Same Moon*

End of Interview

For me, I walked away from this interview with my eyes opened. I had sometimes viewed deployment as time taken away—time my husband wasn't there for me, time my babies didn't get their dad, time we could never get back, time wasted. But hadn't I also seen how my own marriage had been enriched in the time apart? Hadn't I also seen how it made me long for the physical presence of my husband, how it made me want to remember all of who he is and all of the best parts of him? Hadn't I seen how it had made us work harder at knowing each other well, in the absence of being in front of each other? And if I had seen this, could I believe the same could happen for a father and his daughter? Could I trust that this wasn't time wasted but time gained? I could begin to trust. I could begin to see.

SEVENTEEN

UNEXPLAINED

A close friend of mine last year asked me to pray for her friend who went in to wake her eighteen-month-old daughter up for the morning and found her not breathing. This mom began CPR and called 911, trying to pump breath back into her daughter. But her daughter's lifeless body lay still and limp even as the paramedics arrived. She was later diagnosed with sudden unexplained death in children. The explanation: an unexplanation. The doctors and the autopsy reported her daughter to be completely healthy and that this was a rare tragedy. My friend shared this in an effort to support this grieving family, as others had started a GoFundMe to start a charity in this child's name and to help the family financially with funeral costs, meals, and other needs.

I have never forgotten this story. It rocked me to my core. It seemed to axe-slice the posts bouldering the fence of my life, posts that I believed were standing and secure, unmovable. To see the posts gone, damaged, and sliced, the unmovable moved, transformed my perspective. My mornings during deployment consisted typically of waking up to a baby who was screaming or crying, ready to be fed. There was the temptation even as the morning started for me to sigh, to complain, to wish it away or desire it to be different, to feel a wedge of bitterness, a fortitude of frustration. But when I heard this story, I remember tucking Eila close on that space between my neck and shoulder, taking in the sounds of her cooing and the feel of her soft blanket and the curling of her fingers on my back. I remember looking at her and taking her in—the color and shape of her eyes, the silkiness of her skin, the way she liked to kick her feet. This was LIFE and these girls and I got the chance to live it. I spent time thanking God for her, thankful for another day to get to tickle her and watch her squeal with delight, to hold her, to feed her, even to soothe her cries.

Here's what helped me in the worst moments of deployment: remembering to be thankful. Thankful for family and friends who carried us through. Thankful for my two healthy girls. Thankful to simply have breath and life and food and a home. Thankful when my husband is fully present and available to our family. Thankful that we have the communication available to us to talk to him. Thankful to know Jesus.

When all of me felt spent, when the last of all of me felt gone, when the third cup of coffee was made and drunk with no change in energy, I made lists of thankfulness like these:

- Jemma's sweet voice singing the words to "Come Thy Fount" (I sometimes cried when she memorized hymns and seemed to sing them to me when I needed it most. My little two-year-old encourager)
- Jemma reminding me, "Mama, take a deep breath," when she could tell I was overwhelmed
- Eila belly laughing at Jemma being silly (I submit baby laughs as a soother to all that ails)
- Friends who brought over chocolates and flowers from Tony when he couldn't be there on our anniversary and Valentine's Day

- A sister who, on my first day in Texas, made me a bubble bath, took the baby, and said: "Go and enjoy."
- A friend who cleaned the house while I took a shower in the aftermath of the newborn stage
- Ladies' nights that involved extensive talks about how "it really was" and extensive prayer—space to be straightforward, space to lay out my worst thoughts and allow friends to fold them up in truth
- Sisters who did not back down from the task of helping me birth an actual baby
- Friends who had a standing open invitation to join them for Wednesday lunch, giving us something weekly to look forward to, the same friends who sent us home with food from their home almost every time they saw us, just to have another extra meal on hand
- Pizza and movie nights that became a tradition with grandparents
- A stranger on the airplane who was a knowing grandpa and held Eila for me, and offered kind words of encouragement through a long flight to visit family
- Friends who put up little notes of encouragement all throughout my home that I came back to after an all-day plane trip—notes to remind us we were loved and thought of

Could thankfulness be the lens through which I could see deployment differently? Loneliness—a reminder of the one we love, a dirty diaper—a praise that our baby's healthy digestives are working properly, a job that requires separation—financial provision for our family. Could I upend my view to see a different angle, the light shining through the crystalline pattern of my life, tipping it just so in a way that I can see gifts instead of gaps?

The gifts are there—when we have the eyes to see them. Every day is another day to see gifts to thank God for. A healthy body. A mind to think and pray and remember what God has done. Little feet scampering across the wood. Little fingers reaching for snacks. Reaching for my hand. I can thank God for the simple fact of these things. Sometimes our mind can dwell on the negative, creating a negative story of deployment. I had to fight against this by reminding myself of the truth of God's provision. *Yes*, I would remind myself; *See it*, I would remind myself; *Have your eyes open.* Only with our eyes open can we see the beauty.

EIGHTEEN

THERE IS NO ONE MILITARY EXPERIENCE

As I interviewed the women for this book, this fact shined clearly: There is no one military experience. Some might spend four years in the same place and then get out of the Army. Some might spend time overseas in a different culture. Some deployments are three months, some are eleven months. Some are combat situations, some are peacekeeping missions. Not one experience is better than another. All of it can be burdensome and demanding, but all of it can have its rewards and redemptions. My heart for this book is that you may find some insight or a piece of discovery from these women to take with you no matter your experience. You may never feel that anyone totally "gets it." Your experience is your own. But I hope you know that there are many women that have gone before us and many women that will come after that we can lock arms with and learn from as we weather the journey together.

Each of the women interviewed have different personalities. While one woman might say: "Do what you can to help FRG," another woman might say: "Don't sign up for anything—your capacity is diminished." You will have to figure out what works for you and your family. During my deployment, I tried to use that filter: What is best for me and my family? Sometimes getting out of our comfort zone was good—serving others and getting out of the house or our normal routine. But, sometimes, I needed to say no to many things and recognize I couldn't do it all. Sometimes, I had to push myself past my limits when I knew it was best for our family. For example, packing all the girls up alone to go to our church small group felt like running a marathon sometimes. But I knew once I got there, the girls would love playing with their friends and I would have time for some deep, needed conversation and prayer and encouragement. This was worth my putting in the effort.

You have permission to be exactly who you are. Maybe you have a friend who is super loving military life and involved and loves talking about it and getting others involved. You can be like her if you want, but you can also be you. You might have a friend who hates military life and is struggling with finding any positive words about it. That can be you at times too. Or, a combination of them all.

My husband works full-time in the Army Guard currently. Before being full-time, he worked a civilian job and was required to attend "Guard weekends" (typically one weekend a month) and go to needed training at times. Deployment was part of his duties as a guardsman. But life as a wife to a full-time Army guardsman is very different from other kinds of military life. When I talk to other Guard wives, some live far from bases and have little support. Again, there is no one military experience. But, I believe every military family deserves to feel known and heard and understood. I hope that this book will be helpful no matter what your experience or background. Know that the experience of the women interviewed, along with my own experience, is going to be different than yours. Your own down moments or delight moments are going to look and feel different from my own and others.

What is your story? What have been the ups and downs of your military life? How can you begin to share it?

NINETEEN

THE CORN MAZE

B attling my own mind—the exploring, identifying, future telling and future fretting, musing, panicking, brooding thoughts felt like one of those fall festival corn mazes at times. You turn and you're stuck and then a friend helps free you or points you in the right direction, but you wander again and make a wrong turn and then a right one and then maybe you think you've escaped but realize you didn't. You're trapped.

My thoughts were probably the worst things I faced on deployment. My thoughts would run the range of: *Did my kids eat enough vegetables today? I wonder what my friend thinks of the epic catastrophic tantrum Jemma threw. Is my husband awake now? Did I call and make the appointment for Eila's well-child check? Did I turn off the oven? Am I doing a good enough job as a mom? I need to work out my body. When is the last time I worked out? I am so exhausted. How many hours did I sleep last night?*

The "what ifs" and the "I shoulds" and the worry took control of me more than I took control of them on more occasions than I would like to admit. I finally learned to put a word to it: *anxiety*. I can share with the hope of helping others understand that, for me, just even putting a word to it was a huge first step. My husband came home in April from an eleven-month deployment and then had to leave for another two months the following October and November. I felt better mentally when he came home in April, but I really struggled to be myself and be healthy again during those two months he left again in the fall. I felt crippling fear and paralyzing anxiety. I felt dread and guilt and bitterness and anger. Even though it was a shorter time he was gone, my body and mind started going into *panic mode*, a kind of heightened emotional state of survival.

I am a counselor myself and I still needed help. I knew the therapies as a counselor and tried to "counsel my own mind" for far too long. I wish I would have talked to a professional sooner. I wish I wouldn't have felt weak or inferior in asking for help—I wish instead I would have seen this as a strength. I wish I would have talked about it more with others. I wish I wouldn't have been so ashamed to admit the real talk, the real truth, nothing hidden. The more I openly I talked about it in the most honest way I could—not venting about my husband being gone but truly seeking to understand my feelings and my fears and pinpoint my reasons for the fears—the more others came alongside of me to share: "Yes, I have been there too"—and I didn't feel so alone. We feel alone because we chose to be alone. I felt alone because I chose to be alone in my thoughts. My battle with anxiety left me doubtful, teary, and lost. I believed the lie that no one could handle the depth of my thoughts. I believed the lie that I had to face my battle alone.

Nothing can replace professional help if you need it. I encourage this on all accounts. But I want to share some tidbits, some nuggets, that have helped me along the way. Please do not substitute this for seeing your own personal counselor, for giving yourself the grace to reach out to the hand that will lead you through the maze, when you need it. *One step, then another.*

Is there an exit to the corn maze? Maybe the corn maze thinking is what trapped me in the first place. Maybe we are only trapped if we choose to be. If our hearts, minds, souls, our thinking, our dwelling establishes us to be. Can we be freed? How? *One step, then another.*

1. Share the thoughts that cross your mind and become the worst ones. Write them down. Say them out loud. Explore them, journal about them, find their roots. What we feel doesn't mean fact.

    a. A cow eats by *ruminating*, a system of swallowing, re-swallowing, chewing and rechewing. We can't let our thoughts be like this. We have to propel our thoughts forward—process them, get the poo out, and keep moving, allowing ourselves to digest, controlling what we can control in life, and trying to let the rest go to a God who is in control.

2. What practical things can you do to tackle your anxiety? Maybe not an ANSWER. Maybe not the corn-maze EXIT. But a practical next step. Make a list of your worries and see if there is a practical step that you can take for each one, even if it is just to pray.

    a. Personal example: I hated winter driving in Alaska—every time the snow fell, I would start to worry if we would be in a car crash or if my car would slide. I decided to get snow tires put on. It helped ease my anxiety tremendously—believing in the simplicity and safety of a tool that helps tires grip onto the road.

3. Here are some in-the-moment ways to tackle anxiety (for anxiety attacks or when your anxiety is at an ultimate high):

    a. Taking deep, slow breaths—counting down from 100 by 1s, 5s, 10s, maybe 3s to change it up. This engages the math side of your brain and gives the emotional side a stress break.

b. Flexing and then releasing muscles—your calves, arms, fists, your whole body if need be. Again, this gives your brain a chance to focus on your physical body and allows the emotion side to ease up for a moment.

c. Pick three or four of your most favorite spots or moments in your lifetime: When is a time you felt tranquil and relaxed? Imagine all the tastes, smells, feels, sights. Close your eyes and be in those places for a moment. Don't just picture the ocean— smell the salty ocean air, listen to the push and pull of the waves, feel the grains of sand falling softly, the sight of the light blue sky melding into the horizon of the deep blue water, the taste of the mist lingering. Be there in those spots. Write them down, remember them. Come back to them when in a stressful moment—the enveloping entropy being washed and calmed in your own mind, the places you can escape to when needed.

d. Try the 5-4-3-2-1 grounding technique. This focuses on bringing your mind back to reality and helps keep you from winding up and up in your anxiety. The goal is to use your body's senses and say out loud what you experience. Name five things you see around you (sun coming through window, red book), name four things you can feel (soft blanket, gray sweatshirt), name three things you can hear (TV in the background, dog barking), name two things you can smell (if you can't smell anything, name your favorite smells), name one thing you can taste (or name your favorite taste). Try changing up the numbers and senses if you need to—five things to feel, four things to taste, three things to see, etc.

e. Another skill is thumb-to-finger relaxation. Touch your thumb to each knuckle on each finger. Take a deep breath, in and out, as you touch each knuckle.

4. Saying out loud your thoughts and finding healthier thoughts more based on truth to bring yourself back to.

Sometimes we have *repeat phrases*, sentences we go back to, words that create truths we cling to. Those phrases can sometimes be, no matter how hard we grasp onto them and grab them, be untrue in their entirety or half true or we aren't willing ourselves to see the true full picture. In the counseling world, we call these *thinking errors*.

In deployment, I can start thinking in extremes, especially using the terms *always* and *never*. Sometimes our brain holds on to these validations but you can guide yourself back to more truth based statements:

We never get to do normal family things.
VERSUS
Our family time looks different from others, but we love each other and we will learn to do special family things while my husband is gone and when he gets back.

My husband is always gone for work.
VERSUS
Sometimes he is gone for work, but I will learn how to be okay during those times and he will be here eventually.

I am failing as a mom and a wife and in my career.
VERSUS

I am going to have bad days, but that does not mean that I am failing as a whole. I can keep going even past mistakes and hard days. No one is perfect and tomorrow is a new day to start fresh.

5. Big emotional outbursts can start with a trigger—something that ticks something in our brain that causes us to react in a certain way. We can use a set of trigger-tracking questions to journal about and begin to change our thinking as we see patterns. These questions are adapted from the idea of a thought record (Boyes, 2012) and an anger diary (Deffenbacher, 2011).

• Trigger
  What moment caused you to feel a big emotional outburst? What triggered that outburst? A kid yelling? Someone cutting you off? Your husband not having a long time to talk even though you had a lot on your mind?

• Thoughts
  What were you thinking at that moment? What expectations did you have for yourself or others?

• Feelings
  What were you feeling in that moment? Anger can be a secondary emotion often to other first emotions—disappointment, sadness, loss.

• Action
  What were you doing at that moment? How were you acting or behaving?

• Result of Action
  What happened as a result of your actions or behaviors?

• Conflict with Values and Actions
  What is important to you? What are your values and goals as a person? Was your behavior connected to those values

and goals? Is there any conflict or discrepancy between your actions/behaviors and your values/goals?

- <u>What</u> Do You Want to Change?

  Based on your values and goals, what might you want to change or do differently next time? If you could change, how might you change your actions or behaviors?

- <u>When</u> Could You Have Changed?

  At one point in the moment could you have chosen to behave differently? What was your point of change? Was it when your thoughts spiraled, when a certain event started?

- Patterns

  What patterns do you see? Are there certain moments or times during the day or week that are continually stressful? How can you approach those moments differently so as to reduce that trigger and the stress that comes with it?

A personal example of a moment I could have used the trigger tracking for me is a day I felt I took much anger out on my toddler daughter. Sometimes, in parenting, you hold on to certain things that give you security—simple things like what your kids have to eat at meals. During deployment, those security moments got amplified (i.e., my toddler MUST eat and eat healthy foods when I ask because I have to be the best mom I can be during deployment). If I could go back and help myself, it would be to tell myself to offer food and then not worry if my kids didn't eat it. If they throw a fit about the food, they will get hungry later and eat the next meal or snack. They will survive and they will learn to eat food that is offered. But, while my postdeployment and older mother self knows this, my younger mother self didn't know this. I held on to the security that being a good mother meant my kids had to eat lunch before their nap.

On this particular day, my toddler had thrown a fit about leaving the trampoline park and I had held her football style as she kicked and screamed—the "walk of shame"—back to the car as you slowly accept the fact that your toddler will not go willingly. When we got back to the house for lunch, she refused to eat. I finally couldn't take it, slammed my hand on the high chair, yelled "Please just eat your lunch!" and had to take a second out on my front porch to calm down. When I came back, she had picked up pieces of the food and cleaned them up. I told her "I'm sorry." I hugged her, took deep breaths, and (gasp!) put her tired little body to bed even though she didn't have much food in it. We both needed a break. When she woke up, she ate. We survived. But the sting of that day held with me.

Breaking this down into a trigger tracking journal for me would be:

- Trigger

    My trigger was the buildup of Jemma kicking and screaming from the trampoline park to the car and then not eating lunch.

- Thoughts

    I was thinking about how hard deployment was and how I am constantly feeling like I am the only one handling my toddler's tantrums. My expectation for my daughter was that she had to eat every meal and if she didn't, I wasn't doing a good enough job as a mom. I had an expectation of her that she would listen when I asked her to do something. My expectation for myself was that I knew exactly how to handle her tantrums.

- Feelings

    I was feeling sad and guilty that I had slammed my hand on Jemma's highchair, that I had let my anger overtake me. I was feeling frustrated and overwhelmed with caring for a newborn and toddler and having to learn how to handle toddler tantrums on my own. I was feeling alone, forgotten, and incapable.

- Action

I slammed my hand on the highchair, yelled "Please just eat your lunch!" and walked outside to the front porch to regroup and try to think over the situation.

- Result of Action

When I came back, Jemma had cleaned up the pieces of food and was still crying, doing that half hard breathing and crying thing, trying to catch her breath. My head was ringing, and I was crying. I was frustrated with Jemma but ready to try something different and talk with her about what happened.

- Conflict with Values and Actions

It is important to me that I show Jemma patience, love, and kindness no matter what is going on. I want her to also see what it means for me to know Christ and see that in the way I parent her. Me slamming my hand down on the highchair and yelling "Please just eat your lunch!" was not connected to my values and how I want to behave as a parent.

- <u>What</u> Do You Want to <u>Change</u>?

The next time that Jemma refuses to eat or listen, I wanted to have a plan in mind or some phrasing I could use. Learning to use the option of choices helped me: "You can choose to eat your lunch or choose to go to your nap hungry. It's your choice"—this gives the toddler the power to choose and helps them to see the consequences of their choice. I don't want to slam my hand down in anger or yell at my daughter. However, I also know that my kids are going to see me mess up, fail, get angry, sin, and make wrong choices. I prayed a lot after this moment and, while it was a low, it also showed me how I do and do not want to handle my anger and it helped me start to talk to Jemma more about how I was feeling: "I miss your dad. I'm sorry I got angry with you. I want to work on not yelling. Will you forgive me? What are some things you could do differently next time to help me?". In the moments of our failures, our kids also get to see us lean on God and see us bring our needs to Him. Our kids don't need perfect parents—they need Christ more than they need perfect parents. On this day, I am glad that I told Jemma that I was sorry, that we hugged and talked about what happened. This brought restoration to our relationship. It shows her (and reminds me) that we can always talk things over after conflict. I want to keep doing that because I value that.

- <u>When</u> Could You Have Changed?
  The moment that Jemma kept refusing food was my "moment or point of change."

- Patterns
  This trigger-tracking journal helps us to see patterns of behavior or particular moments of stress during the day that we could brainstorm different solutions for a better outcome in which we can respond based on our values. This journal helped me to see that mealtimes, transition times such as when we leave places, and times when Jemma is repeating the same phrase over and over were trigger patterns for me and I was responding to those triggers in a way that I wanted to change.

The high level of expectation we put on ourselves and others can be unrealistic. When expectations are unmet, we can feel disappointed and defeated. Learning to change our expectations is important. My daughter was two at the time. Two-year-olds are realistically going to have tantrums, refuse to do things, fight boundaries, and disobey. Realistically, I am not going to always know how to respond. I can try different parenting methods and keep learning. I can try new things and start fresh. But every day will bring new challenges, especially with a two-year- old. Disappointment can be expectations unmet, and expectations re- moved can be disappointment removed.

6. Another tool is the ABCDE way of outlining and discover- ing our thinking from the rational emotive behavior thera- py created by Albert Ellis (Ellis, 2011).

A—Activating Event

What happened that initiated my stress or anxiety? What did I do? What did others do? What was I feeling?

B—Beliefs

What am I believing or thinking about the event? What phrases were running through my head? What do I believe about myself surrounding what happened?

C—Consequences

How did I behave or act because of my beliefs? What am I feeling because of my beliefs?

D—Disputing the Irrational Beliefs

Is my belief true? Is my belief not true? If it is not true, how can I change it to be true? If you are someone who believes in God, filter your thoughts through God's Word and God's view of you.

E—Effective New Beliefs to Replace the Irrational Ones

If my belief was not true, how can I change it to be true? How can I change what I believe about myself and what is true about myself?

How might this look during deployment? Here is a made up example but could definitely be a real one for me.

A—The Activating Event

The refrigerator breaks and turns off, giving me limited time to find a solution before all the food goes bad at the same time the baby is screaming and my toddler is throwing a tantrum about not getting the yogurt she wanted but I am staring at the fridge wondering what to do, knowing that I will be facing all of this alone because my husband is overseas. Because of the time difference, I will not be able to talk to him until around five in the evening.

B—Beliefs

My beliefs or inner thoughts might be: *I cannot handle this. I am going to lose my mind. I cannot do this.*

C—Consequences

The consequences of those beliefs might be that I get frustrated in anger at my toddler and yell at her to stop crying. When she doesn't and probably keeps crying because of my yelling, maybe I spank her out of anger and then feel guilty about spanking her because the fridge is really what set me off but at the same time her tantrum is something that I want to handle better. Then, maybe, I start crying because of the guilt and the overwhelming feeling of helplessness and the fact that the baby has been crying for the last ten minutes and everyone is still hungry because I don't want to open the fridge more and risk the food going bad.

D—Disputing the Irrational Beliefs

How do I begin to start over here? The first step is realizing that the mind is where choices, beliefs, and behaviors begin. The first step is trying to figure out what beliefs led to the consequences. It started with: "I cannot handle this" and led to "I am going to lose my mind" and then finished with "I cannot do this." Then those thoughts began to permeate my reality as I allowed them to. My thoughts became my truth because I let them be. I have to begin to question my beliefs and statements—Are they true? Are they rational?

E—Effective New Beliefs to Replace the Irrational Ones

Instead, I could have thought: "This is hard, but I can handle this" and then led to "I am going to take one thought, one step, one moment at a time" and then finished with "I can do this." Then, I could have taken a deep breath and fed the baby. I could have given my daughter a time-out, giving both myself and her a break. After talking to her about the tantrum, I could have fed her a snack, realizing that opening the fridge one time would be fine while I figured out what to do. I could have then called the repairman and set a time for when he could come over. In the meantime, I could have transferred some items to the freezer. I could have then called to ask a friend or family to babysit (realizing it is an overwhelming day) and looked at possible fridge options in case the fridge couldn't be fixed.

The "could haves" are life and they will keep happening. It's being human—knowing you could have worked through your mind, your thoughts, your actions differently. But the ABCDE tool helps to track your thinking. Thoughts led to behaviors. What we do starts with what we think. As we transform our thinking, we can change our actions.

Try to identify the real fears you have, the root issue of your anxiety. Is my real fear that we won't have enough food? Once you know this fear, try to tackle this fear: I will take a deep breath and order a pizza. There are others who love us who can help us if our food goes bad. Is my fear that I won't be able handle all the tasks that need to be done? I can take the tasks one step at a time and ask for help when I need it. Maybe my fear is deeper than that though. Maybe my fear, ultimately, is: Are my kids going to be taken care of in the right ways during deployment, if deployment feels like the fridge breaking and one thing after the other that I have to take care of that is not them? Answer this fear with truth: All I can do is the best I can do. I am a mom who loves my children deeply and I will care for them in the best ways I can and trust that in my failings, God will care for them.

Me being in the counseling chair, being counseled was grounding, humbling, and, for me, courageous. My own counseling looked like a lot of me expressing my hurts, learning to heal from my hurts, learning that I could work on healing my own hurts instead of expecting others to cater to my hurts, learning that I could explore forgiveness on my own instead of expecting a certain phrase or reaction or understanding from others, learning why I was hurt, and more healing from my hurts. Every session brought a small, slight change, a glimmer of new perspective, specks of revelation like a clean rag running over dusty parts of my heart that had been in hiding and then wiping them again as dust began to form. Those parts of my heart were dusted off, brought forth in the light and began to beat again.

Sometimes, the "thinking error thoughts" have you stuck. That was me at times. I am a counselor. I know the theories. I am a believer who loves Jesus deeply. I have the tools. And still I get stuck. There you find me—curled up in a ball, crying, begging, demanding, protesting, worrying, wondering, despairing. There you find me—entirely in the corn maze—head down, tears rolling, not moving, not trying. There you find me—the actual task of putting one foot in front of the other too much. The actual task of attempting to find the exit too much.

How do you move forward from the stuck place? Do I expect myself to move or others to find me?

Believe the truth that there is no thought too dark or too deep or too dangerous to say out loud to someone else. Don't forget to BE alive—to look up and experience. Yes, you are in a corn maze. But what else is around? Smell the grass and the hedges and the sweat of others working to find their way out too. Touch the blades of the grass, the dew of the autumn morning damp all around. You can taste it—the air crisp and clear, the fireweed changing from purple to red. You can see it—the mountains jagged and just, pointed and proud—the snow just starting to pile at the top, the blues and greens mixed with the reds and oranges and pinks of fall. I can look around and feel and experience nature beckoning and calling, inviting me out of the maze and back into what the world has to offer, back into what God has for me each day, back into the gifts of each day.

Anxiety, I found for me, was wound up in obsessing over what could be or what has been—worry over my parenting in the past or how the deployment might affect my kids in the future, how I handled a conversation with someone or conflict, if Tony was okay or what it would look like when he returned. What I allowed anxiety to take from me was the present. What the future would hold, I still have to learn to accept, can be focused on at a later time in the future when the time comes to focus on it. For now, I have to take in fully all that I have and all that I can be in the right now—two wildly energetic girls, deep friendships, mountains to explore, adventures to discover through the eyes of a two-year-old and a newborn.

I don't believe the phrase: God never gives you more than you can handle. A newborn and a two-year-old and eleven months of my husband being away WAS too much for me to handle. But it wasn't too much for God to handle, when I allowed Him to—when I realized it was all His to guide me through, to be right there with me in, to walk with me in each step and care for me in the deepest lows. This isn't a cure or an immediate solution or a fix all—but it is a truth that can be a salve to the wounds of loneliness, the pit of anxiety, the drowning self-pity that I can sometimes find myself in. I had to whisper it, share it, discuss it, yell it, wonder in it at times. I had to say it in the car with screaming kids in their car seats: "God, you are here. You never leave me nor forsake me. You have not left me. I am not alone. You care for me in this. You are here." I had to say it to my own mind, my self-talk, my corn maze that felt inescapable, the words out loud, bouncing off the tall barrels of hay that I thought I couldn't see over: "Yes, God you are here, even in the stuck place."

TWENTY

THE ONE STEP

I was never a "mountain person." But then, I moved to Alaska ten years ago. Our town is alive with the delight in the conquering of a peak, the relish of the victory of the summit. The mountains stare at you, wondering, waiting, daring, summoning. *Who are you?* they seem to whisper. As someone who grew up in Texas, I was cautious about the mountains, curious, unsure. My relationship with them has oscillated between serenity and rage. I have trudged through mud, snow, ice, creeks, and rocks trying to keep up with the mountain masters. I have endured bloody knees, bug bites, skin rashes, thirst, hunger, at times carrying twenty-to-thirty-pound toddlers on my back. There is part of me that wants to change the cool saying from "The mountains are calling and I must go" to "The mountains are calling and I should consider saying no."

I have questioned what it's all about, why there is an addiction to this nature conquest and why everyone drinks the Kool-Aid of it. *I can't do this*, I think. I have to turn back. NOT worth it. I have been on hikes with false peaks. I didn't know that was a thing until I moved here. You think you've made it to the top but then you have more to go, sometimes A LOT more to go.

I am not going to pretend that I am some kind of magical mountaineer. I don't always get to the tippy top. I have two kids often with me—who need snacks and drinks and who complain sometimes the entire way. I have turned around at times. But I have also sat on a mountain ridge, apex achieved, looking at crown upon crest upon cap for miles, a vast, endless display of savage, rugged splendor.

The more steps you take, the more stunning the view, the more you can see how far you've come, maybe even the parking lot where you can see the tiny car that you took that first step out of. For me in the mountains and for me on deployment, those steps were everything. *One step, then another.* They meant I was moving forward. The steps matter. Maybe, some days you can't see the forward progress. Maybe, some days it feels like a lot of moving back. Maybe, some days you need to sit down on the trail, grab a snack, and a drink and rest.

Fresh ideas can help. This chapter is dedicated to those "one steps." Use what follows here to try another step, to get the momentum to keep going. Take ideas from some things that practically helped me. Maybe some will work for you but maybe some won't. Take what works. Use it to take your *one step, then another.*

Plan A, Plan B, and also Plan A+ and Plan A-

When you have an expectation and a vision about the way things should go and they don't go that way, this is where you can feel devastated or distraught. I had to learn to have my plan A and to not be upset about not getting plan A, but make a plan B (which we could maybe even call plan A- or plan A+), a plan that I was also equally as excited for. Because I had a newborn during deployment, napping and sleep meant so much to me. I had to learn to let go of how much value I put on sleep and not feel like I was going to completely lose it if I didn't get the sleep I wanted or imagined or needed. I had to make a plan A (normally sleep) and a plan B (maybe plan A- or plan A+): If the baby wakes up during nap time, then I won't cry or be angry or give up feeling like I can't "mom" the rest of the day. Instead, I will use that time to: call a friend, do dishes, or meal plan. Or maybe, I will use that time to watch a completely pointless show or eat a snack or do a workout while the babe crawls around on the floor next to me. Whatever the plan was, I had to have one ready so that when plan A went awry (which it often did), plan B was kind of more like plan A- or maybe even plan A+ (just as thrilling or better than plan A would have been, something I could look forward to).

Laughter and Play

On a very rare moment that I got to sit down with my sister face-to-face during the deployment, she asked me how it was really going and how I was really doing. I remember telling her that one thing had become very important for us and that was to laugh and play every day. In the seriousness of deployment, in the absolute sucking drain of it, I didn't want to lose being purely present with my kids, and I didn't want to lose the joy of being with them. Now, let's be real. Some days you are going to need a break. And, some days, it does NOT feel like joy. And it is okay to express this and care for yourself in those moments. But I would try to bring as much glee and giggles into our lives as I could. It kept my spirits high and my heart light.

Some ways I would practically do this included: tickle fights, bubbles, dance parties, painting, popcorn and movies in bed, hide and seek, new bath toys, being outside, going to community events like the fair or the market, fire pits and marshmallows, making play dates and park dates with friends, baking together, or doing holiday themed activities together (Easter egg hunts, pumpkin patches). When my kids were smiling and laughing, I was too! I think having this mindset helped me to focus on the right things during deployment. Sometimes, we can get caught up in the busyness, the day-to-day, the errands and the necessities, and the to-do lists. I had to stop and ask during deployment (and still have to ask): Did I sit and play with my kids today? Not just drop them off at a sport or a class or do school things. Did I actually PLAY? Did I enjoy them today? If the answer is no, I knew even if I felt tired, even if it felt impossible, that the play would fill me up in the right ways and would probably fill my kids up too.

Neighbors

I would try to think of activities that would involve caring for our neighbors or people we knew were in need but in simple and easy ways that my kids could join me in doing. We would take valentine cards and candies to our neighbors or decorate thank you cards for our babysitters or friends. As others I interviewed said, the more you think of others, the less you are focused on yourself and that can be a welcome distraction from the woes of deployment.

Find Ways to Do What You Love

Don't let the military keep you from doing what you love, but know that doing what you love may look different for you than it does for others you know. I completed an entire interview for this book while my kids took a bath. I was taking one baby out, wrapping her in a towel, putting lotion on her, doing all the bath things while also holding a phone and trying to talk military life with a friend. There is the temptation to feel like you never get to do what you love, have free time or a social life. Be creative and don't let the constraints of military life stop you. Sure, the interview would have been better if I could have sat across from this friend at a coffee shop, listening with no kids to attend to. But military life is my reality. My husband is gone a lot. That truth is something I have to face and overcome and find ways to take care of myself in the midst of. Writing is one of those things for me, so I make it work the best way I can, even when it might look absolutely bonkers.

Find Ways for You Both to Do What You Love

When your loved one comes back, you and your loved one will still need time for you both to do things that you love. Sometimes, I put a lot of pressure on Tony that since we don't get to see him a lot, his time at home needs to look a certain way (house projects, time with the kids, time with me, etc.). I don't allow time for him to rest at times because I have this obsession that the time is so limited. This puts unneeded stress on us both. It is actually vital for Tony to have guilt-free time to do things he enjoys. This allows him to feel refreshed and energized to do the needed things and the same is true for me. Speak up when you need to ask for time away and be willing to give guilt-free time away to your loved one when needed too. Be reasonable in your asking time with each other but also be open and willing to compromise to see how you can both fit time in to do this.

All the Feels

When the emotions come out, they give us insight into what's really going on inside of ourselves. When we get angry, sad, or frustrated, it is a chance for us to not hide our feelings but talk to our creator, our friends, our counselor, or our own selves about them.

If something irks you, ask yourself: What was it about that comment on the phone call that made me feel that feeling in a big way? Maybe, you won't be able to voice even the feeling or why it made you feel inferior or tired or unloved in the moment. But consider different ways you could try saying or doing something in the future or have your partner or kids try saying or doing different things to help you with the big emotions.

"When you said the kids seem crazy tonight, that made me feel like you don't think I am doing a good job here at home during the deployment. I know you probably didn't mean it like that, so can you try starting by asking how I am doing next time?"

Invite your deployed loved one to do the same. They might feel really lonely at times. Invite them to share that. "I felt really sad watching that video of our kids at the park today." Invite them to share when they feel you have said or done something hurtful and how you might phrase it differently or try something different next time. He might say: "It hurt when you said I am missing out on a lot because I really do want to be there. Could you try saying instead: 'I know you wish you could have been there for the recital today. We thought about you and missed you.'" Consider each other's feelings and continue to work at loving each other well even from far away. Know that you won't be perfect at it but make it your goal to keep trying, to learn from ways you didn't understand each other well and to work towards making it better next time.

There is no one "doing it better" or "doing the harder work" who gets an out for saying hurtful things (even though it may not feel like this at times). You're still in a relationship and working on that relationship in a deployment. Even when it doesn't feel like you are in the wrong, it is helpful in conflict to consider your part and your responsibility in that conflict. Consider: Could you try calling at a different time? Could you try leading with a question instead of a demand? Be willing to see your part even when the emotions are running high.

Model this for kids if needed. Help your kids to voice their feelings and also be willing to own your part as a parent. I have had to apologize to my kids at times: "Hey, I am sorry that I yelled like that at you. I really miss daddy right now and it makes me sad and frustrated sometimes. Will you forgive me?" Hug, kiss, and, if the child can understand, explain how they can help next time or ask them what they think they could do differently: "It's my fault that I yelled, but what could you try differently that would help next time?" If kids can't think of something, tell them how: "It would help me if you did not say my name over and over when you need me, and I am helping your baby sister. Next time, come up to me and when I am done helping Eila, you can ask me once what you need."

The Twenty-Minute Timer

I have used this statement often in my life: *You can do anything for twenty minutes.* During deployment, you are the only parent, house cleaner, dog poop picker upper, family communicator, the only everything. When I would stare at a sink full of dishes or a toddler throwing a massive tantrum or a pile of mail that needed to be sorted, try starting a twenty- minute timer. Take a deep breath, maybe two, maybe three, say a prayer, steady yourself and get to work. Sometimes, the idea of twenty minutes will get you started and you will be able to keep going and finish the project. Maybe, it will be enough just to take that *one step, then another.* Maybe, it will be enough for the tantrum to end and you to gain some sanity.

Spending Time Alone with Your Kiddo When Needed

Sometimes your kids need time alone with you without other distractions or your other kids around. I know with Jemma, my two-year-old at the time, there were a couple occasions that I was able to take her out and spend some special time alone with her—just me and her—doing things she loved, asking her about her favorite things, giving her some needed attention. Honestly, I wish I would have set aside time for this more than I did. With a parent gone, one-on-one time can be crucial. My aunt offered to watch my newborn after we both discussed the tantrums Jemma was having. It makes sense looking back—Jemma had been adapting to her dad being gone and a newborn in the house, two giant changes in her life. On another occasion, I noticed that Jemma and I were butting heads and I asked a friend to watch Eila, our three-month- old at the time, so Jemma and I could go to an indoor waterpark. It was a memory that I treasure to this day—a whole morning of time just the two of us splashing, Jemma grinning ear to ear as we floated in a tube in the wave pool. It was a reset button, and I was glad we pushed it.

Exercise and Eating Healthy and Getting Outside

It feels like "just another thing to do" when I start talking exercise and eating healthy and getting outside. I know because I've been there—those times, it makes me want to cry just thinking about how completely far off I am from where I would like to be in those areas. *One step, then another.* For me, I am honestly not a person who is very good at these things in the first place. But during deployment, when I was learning to try to be the best I could be so I could be the best I could be for my kids and support my husband, making healthy goals, even if I wasn't perfect at it (because who is?), exercise and eating healthy and getting outside truly did help me. Exercise can be simple—taking your kids on a walk in the stroller or running around with your dog at the park. Eating healthy can look like incorporating new fruits and vegetables into your diet and talking about those recipes or having your kids help you cook as quality time together. Getting outside can be the absolute best antidote to the poison that the feelings of deployment can bring. But all of these things can also feel overwhelmingly not simple, and I get this too. I found that using an app that has the workouts set up and ready to go was helpful (one click and you can do it from your own home)—I could do this while my kids watched a show or whenever I could fit it in. Exercise improved my sleep—those nights when my mind would linger on some image of someone breaking in or my parenting failures or other creeping thoughts (all the very worst thoughts seem to come at night or in the shower)—exercise brought exhaustion and exhaustion brought deep sleep.

It Is the Same and It Is Different

There can be two approaches to times when your loved one is away: (1) Setting a routine you stick to and helping that be the same when your loved one gets back, and (2) knowing that it will look different when they are gone and incorporating some special different things you do when he is gone or maybe a combination of the two. Explore this contrast—What things can you keep the same to maintain structure and what things are going to look different? How can you see the beauty in the difference of this season? Many interviewees mentioned unique opportunities—more time to spend with friends or special events just for you and the kids. How could this time be embraced in its differences and how can routine be embraced for you and your family?

He Won't Be Your Savior When He's Home and All the Problems Won't Disappear
　　and
If He Was Home, You'd Still Need to Work on Issues

Read that again, slowly, and maybe say it out loud. These statements were something I had to process as I prepared for my husband's arrival home. What expectations did I unknowingly (or possibly knowingly) put on him for when he came home? Were those expectations realistic? If you haven't heard of the "honeymoon period," it is a time when your deployed loved one comes home and it feels like this beautiful, rainbow, unicorns, and confetti moment. He's back and he is the best thing in the world—everything is right again. And in some ways, it is. But the reality is, it won't be. Or, eventually, it won't. Problems that have been there all along will rear their ugly heads again. The underlying conflicts that have been kept at bay will come out and the feelings you have been holding down for months will surface.

When my husband was gone, I tried to remind myself of this—he can't be my savior, the solution, the answer—before, during, or after deployment. If I believe that he will be, I will be disappointed, frustrated, and dissatisfied. I think the "thinking error" can be that the kids will stop misbehaving, all the house projects will get done, and all the help and support I need will be here when he gets here. But life is a blend of imperfection, mistakes, of trying and failing, and of learning and trying again. Your loved one will be who they are when they left—just a person trying and failing and learning and trying again—the person you loved, but also a person who has been changed and transformed by new experiences. Welcome them for who they are, with all the changes, and know that they will step into life with you again, but they won't be the answer to all the problems—and putting this much weight on them, the pounds and pounds of expectation, will cause them to crumble.

Know When to Call in Support

Are you financially able to hire someone to help you out in certain areas? Lawn mowing, house cleaning, etc. I used Instacart often to deliver groceries during deployment and restaurant food delivery services, such as Grubhub, Uber Eats, or DoorDash.

Sometimes, having one less thing to do or worry about, one less thing on your list, helps big time. Maybe it won't be forever; maybe it's just this season of deployment. It is okay to ask for those small tokens of assistance.

Being in Your Own Pond

I had to learn to "be in my own pond" during deployment. Imagine you are in a small circular pond—tranquil, calm, fish splashing, birds chirping, the sunshine reflecting on the water. I had to learn tools to be okay on my own in my own pond—not needing actions from others to be okay. We don't need others to change in order to be okay in our own pond. It's the reminder that we are the ones who make our choices and decisions. If we get angry, it's not another person's fault no matter what they did. If we get angry, we have a choice to completely lose it or to work on expressing that anger in a healthier way. If our deployed loved one forgets to ask about our day or forgets to call at the time they said they would, we have the right to express how we feel, but we also have to learn how to be okay within our own pond. Take a deep breath and be okay in your pond. You don't have to join up with a river or an ocean or a lake. You don't need the saltwater or the rapids or the waterfalls. You are okay in your pond.

Our happiness and peace and "okayness" can't depend on the actions of others. We have to learn to determine it within ourselves and in knowing God. I have spent too much energy in my life at times being frustrated with others—demanding change or protesting when people aren't treating me the way I think they should. This can be so exhausting (and so focused on blaming others and not on what I can do)! I have learned to work on my responsibility in a situation—to do what I can and leave it at that. I can't constantly blame others for how I feel or look to others for my own "okayness." Others around me can work on needed change in their lives (because no one is perfect and everyone has faults), but I also have much to work on! The pond visual is a way to practice not allowing others to determine my "okayness"—not being devastated and completely focused on the disappointment others might bring, but to focus on what I can control—my response to others and my own actions. I can't control the actions of others, so I can't spend hours of energy trying to do this. I can learn to walk securely with this knowledge, facing whatever may come my way and learning to limit the expectations I push on to others, not forcing their actions to be what makes me okay but letting my own actions and thoughts be what makes me okay, letting God in and helping Him transform my thoughts. As someone who loves Jesus, I am able to carry within my own pond the knowledge that I am loved, cared for, and known by the God of the universe.

Within that pond, I can still speak up when I am hurt or talk with others about changing their actions when they hurt me. But if they don't (and, sometimes, okay, often, people won't and may continue hurting and disappointing you), I am still okay.

I am in a place now where I am learning to embrace the career my husband has chosen. Instead of complaining or wishing it was different, I am working on tools I can use in my own thinking and heart to help take on the times he will be away with less anxiety. I am learning to not wish it to change but to understand it and accept it. As I have walked in this new mindset, I am able to take on the future with more confidence whatever it may look like.

Draw from the Strength of Hard Moments in Your Life

Remember moments in your life that you have seen God provide, that you saw the strength of God and the strength you had in you. Imagine them vividly. Remind yourself that God is with you in the here and now, in these hard moments. Make a list if you need to—How has God shown Himself to you in the hard moments of your life?

"I will remember the deeds of the Lord; yes, I will remember your wonders of old." (Psalm 77:11)

"I remember the days of old; I meditate on all that you have done; I ponder the work of your hands." (Psalm 143:5)

For me, turning to God in the hardest moments gave me comfort more than anything the world could ever offer. There is so much hope and peace found in knowing your creator. Remind yourself of how faithful God is and remind yourself of how He will show His faithfulness to you again and again, even in the unknown future.

TWENTY-ONE

THE PENDULUM

"I think we should let her cry it out."
"I want her to finish her food before getting down."
"She needs to learn to play on her own."

My initial feelings when parenting statements are made from my husband after a length of time he has been away: that prickling feeling, the spikes going up. Enter feelings even of resentment, bitterness, feelings of inferiority, feeling less than, feeling like I didn't do it well, feeling like I failed and this is being pointed out.

When Tony came back from deployment, I had to learn to let him care for the kids in the way he thought best and to give worth to his opinion, even though it felt like he didn't have the right to. Even though he was gone for so long, he is still their dad, and he does get to share his thoughts and hopes and concerns. They need that and I need that, even though the adjustment can feel excruciating at times. I knew we needed him, although sometimes I felt like I was doing the better job and this can be a difficult thing to work through on deployments and after. My husband helped transition my daughter from a crib to a toddler bed, took the pacifier away, and helped potty train my daughter. Those were all things I didn't feel I had the capacity to do while he was gone.

They felt impossible while he was gone and he made them possible. Recognize the help and collaborate to be a team—voice to your partner when you see how they help. Your partner probably needs this reassurance just as it is good for you to say it out loud. Let them know that you need encouragement too—to be reminded that you did well and that your partner is thankful for you and what you have done and that making adjustments doesn't mean you didn't do it well while your loved one was away. I like to say we are all a little brighter, bolder, and better when my husband is here—and I have to remind myself of that truth—because it is true, even if it doesn't feel that way sometimes.

I think it is normal to want time away when your partner gets back, to ask for breaks from kids or breaks in general, but maybe to want control over what that break looks like with kids. *I wouldn't discipline like that, I wouldn't let them watch that much TV or eat that,* you might think. But your partner is stepping into this role again. They are a different person with different ideas, a needed component in your family life. It is not good for kids to triangulate or use one parent against the other (i.e., "Mom lets us do this . . ." or "Dad does it this way . . ."), but it is good for kids to have different authorities who try things in different ways. Be on the same team about major things, but also consider your partner's perspective. Listen and consider different methods and, also, when you are taking time away, try to completely step back and allow your partner to fully take over. You need time away and they will need to learn to be the solo parent too.

Yes, it is hard to let go of control when we think parenting should look a certain way, and especially when we have done it by ourselves for a long time, but it is also needed for you to get time away to yourself and, to be able to do this, you will have to learn to relinquish control of it looking a certain way.

For me during deployment, there was a pendulum swing with my parenting thinking at times. Sometimes I would feel inadequate, and swing to the side of the idea that I was worthless, failing as a mom, feeling self-conscious about what I couldn't do or didn't have the ability to do as a solo parenting mom. Those thoughts would creep in: *I am a terrible mom. My kids ate Cheetos all day or watched three hours of TV or had the worst behavior.* In those moments, we need the reminder: *I am a loving mom.* Maybe you need to say it out loud or make a list: I do feed my kids, show them affection, take them outside, read to them, care about them eating healthy foods, take them to the doctor, and care about them spiritually. It is good to remind yourself what you do practically to care for your kids. Reminders of what you do for them can help.

Ultimately, we need the reminder that our identity and who we are has to be found in Christ. If who we are is defined by our kids' behavior or how many Cheetos we ate or they ate or how many spankings we did or didn't give, then we are doomed! Luckily, we can turn back to what God says about who we are: that we are loved by the God of the universe and that love is not given based on performance or our own behavior as a mom or wife or friend or house cleaner, it is given based on what Jesus did for us on the cross. We are loved because we are daughters and sons of God, not because of what we have done.

Then, there is the other pendulum swing—swinging to the side of pride. This is what creeps in when we feel like WE did all the right things during deployment, that our partner/fiancé/husband doesn't have a clue and that we are always going to be the better parent. The thoughts we might have here are: *I am the best parent, my partner doesn't know what they are doing.* In these moments, I have learned to try to let go and allow my husband to share in parenting in the way he would like to. We need to remind ourselves of the times that we too aren't perfect as parents—that we too have responded out of anger or tiredness or fed them three cupcakes or chose our own convenience over their needs.

In pride, we also need to find our identity in Jesus—that we aren't the BEST or BETTER parent (remind yourself of times when your partner has helped and is needed and is such a necessary component of your family), that ultimately the ability to love our kids well is God in us loving them and that we do not get extra points with God for being a good mom, but Jesus is the one who scored the points of "earning" for us. We can stop trying to be perfect in every area of our life, including parenting, and work on being the best we can be, knowing it won't be perfection. We can give our partner coming back from deployment grace and understanding, freedom to parent and make mistakes along the way, freedom to learn to be a parent the way they think is best.

I imagine sometimes God holding the pendulum, with us swinging from one side to the other, expending our energy relentlessly on either side. He waits patiently, steadfast, faithful, ready for us to stop swinging, waiting for us to stop moving, to just rest, to be held.

Mom Guilt and Just Plain Guilt

Guilt comes from the regret of not doing something the way we thought we should, from the idea that we should or have to be perfect—maybe, it's how we think we should have parented or acted, the "right way." I have dwelled deeply on this at times—sat restless in guilt, discontent, lodged in my thoughts. But guilt also stems from the idea that we think we must be perfect. We aren't perfect. We can't expect to be—in the past, now, or in the future. All we can do is accept that we have made mistakes and work on ways to be better every day- and to invite Jesus to help us do this.

Admitting You Are Flawed: Sin

I hate the word *sin* because it is loaded. SIN. *Sin* sounds icky, gross, shameful. Isn't that a word for people who have done really terrible things—things we don't speak of?

The nagging questions we ask linger in life: Am I a good person? Am I a bad person? Am I just kind of . . . in the middle? The lists and the scales of motherhood jump in my mind. Can't we offer evidence either way? Can't we linger in our own "good mothering" or just overall "goodness"—thinking of how perfectly our children slept, ate, performed, and played seemingly because of us? How do we define being a good mother? And where does it end? Do we measure it by our kid sharing at the playground or eating their veggies? Do we measure it by them earning the good citizenship award at the elementary assembly? Or, maybe, it's when they get into an Ivy League school or get a certain SAT score? Is it when they get married? How do we know when, finally, we can say we are a good mother?

And can't we argue the opposite way? Can't we say that we are a bad mother? Couldn't we, like in a courtroom, offer the evidence to show how poor our parenting is? What about the epic meltdown in the store when my kid knocked over twelve boxes of mac 'n' cheese? What about when my daughter straight up slapped her sister for no reason at all? Or when the constant whining and pestering and questions became too much and we snapped as a mom and we yelled at our kids, shutting them down, and we know we took it too far? Couldn't the weight of these many moments heavily outweigh the weights of the good, earning me the title of "Bad Mom" for sure?

I don't remember teaching Jemma to slap Eila. She just did it. Left a red mark on that unknowing, unready little one-year-old's face. This is sin nature: the awful truth that we don't really want to encounter. We are born with the desire to do the opposite of good. Because the truth about *sin* is that it is a word that all of us can claim but none of us want to. None of us are perfect. Which means we sin. We can mourn it and moan about it, we can pretend we don't care about how it affects ourselves and others (or, we may be in a place where we can pretend no longer and the devastating effects of it overtake us). But it is still there whether we accept the truth of it or not: sin. That icky word *sin* that, if we are truly honest, describes us.

So how do we make sense of the scales, the weights, the pendulum swing? For me, I found the answer at a river.

TWENTY-TWO

THE RIVER

Recognizing You Can't Do It on Your Own: We Need God

"Mama, I cleaned it," Jemma said quietly, pointing to the bits of food that had splattered around the highchair, counter, and floor after I had slammed my hand down in frustration in front of her.

I knew it on the front porch after I had slammed my hand down on Jemma's highchair. It's not just that I couldn't do it all. It's that when I tried to, I failed. Enter emotions: anger (at myself and my toddler), sadness (that my husband wasn't here), fear (that this deployment and my lack of ability to overcome all of its cascading effects would drastically affect myself and my kids). We need something more than ourselves. We are lacking. If deployment has taught me anything, it is the clearest possible vision of my need. When I tried to muster up to face it on my own, to put on a brave face, to have it altogether, I failed. Repeatedly.

Understanding What Jesus Has Done: The Cross

It was at a river the summer after eighth grade that I vividly remember feeling and knowing the presence of God. Having gone to church on Sundays, I had heard it before: Jesus died on the cross for you. He took your sins, the wrong things you have done, and he took on the penalty of sin for you. He was a sacrifice, a blameless man who took on blame, a perfect man who took on imperfection. In doing this, Jesus gave us life after death—a gift we can't earn and don't deserve—but a gift we so lavishly get to take part in because of the love of God.

That March, my dad passed away suddenly. I don't think I truly understood that death really could happen until that March. Death was something that happened to old people, right? You had time to prepare for death, right? No, those truths were unraveling before my eyes and the simple fact of it was blaring: He was gone. My dad: a kind, hardworking, family man. My dad: A man who spent hours taking my sister and I to the library, the park, the museum, our sports events; a man who loved being a dad, not because he should or had to, but because he loved us. He was gone. Death was real.

I remember that river: The water weaving and ribboning, the harsh pulse of it beating against the rocks, pushing, roaring, scraping, eroding. I sat on a boulder, looking down at its infinite rush, the trickling, the splashing. It seemed to ask: *Will you stay here or will you keep moving?* The rest of the world had kept moving around me. The river wasn't forcing me as I felt the rest of the world was. The river let me be myself. It was soothing to sit on the rock. There was something easy and knowing in the movement forward. *You can do it*, it said.

I remember that day because it felt like the first time I had cried about my dad dying. I'm sure I had welled up tears at the funeral, slow tears when I felt like loved ones wanted me to have them, drops of tears at the edges of my eyes at the mention of my dad's death. But, this time, at the river—I let it out freely and fully. I wept, I sobbed, the kind where you start almost choking with the snot coming out your nostrils. I asked God why it had to happen. I asked God if He was real. I asked God why death was real. I asked

God if I could be angry. I remember my tears flowing down my cheeks, landing drip drop onto the rapids. The river let me ask the questions I really wanted to, the ones that had been hidden for months, the ones I felt like I wasn't supposed to ask but wanted to. Who will be my dad? I remember asking. It felt like the answer had been there all along: *I will.*

I remember feeling a pull around me that night: what felt like a blanket or a tight squeeze. It has only happened that once in my life—the closest I have ever felt to God—a physical, knowing comfort. There I was: a thirteen-year-old, arms around my knees, my misty eyes melting into the mist of the river, and I didn't feel alone. My relationship with God and with Jesus started that night and I was hungry for it—hungry for reading my Bible, hungry for knowing the truth. I think, even if you hear it a thousand times in church, it has to be your own relationship. It has to be your decision and you have to be ready. No one can force you to be ready. And that night, I was.

TWENTY-THREE

THE LIGHT

"Why do I love you?" I ask my daughter as I walk into her room after her refusing to put her clothes on for the day.

"Because I am your daughter." I nod and hug her, tears streaming from both of our eyes. "I love you and part of my job is to teach you right and wrong. You are my daughter, I love you no matter what you do. But when you make certain choices, I have to give you consequences."

When my husband and I were getting marriage counseling, we had a mentor who explained how he and his wife disciplined their kids. When their kids do something wrong, they pull the child away to speak separately—they talk about consequences and give them if needed, but they also ask: "Why do I love you?" The child can learn to answer: "Because I am your daughter." Or, "Because I am your son." As the parent, you can then explain the Gospel: "Yes, I love because you are my daughter (or son). Your behavior—good or bad—is not what determines my love for you. I love you because you are mine." Then, you can hug your child and have restoration after a consequence if needed. The hug doesn't say, "What you did was okay." Instead it says: "I love you no matter what choice you make. I won't keep punishing you after I give you the consequence. We can move on from this in forgiveness and grace."

This visual is so powerful in its representation of the Gospel—and so needed for me as a mom. I have used this method of discipline as a parent and it has been as much for me as it is for my kids. A reminder for me of the love God has for me just as much as a reminder for my kids.

Responding by Relationship Not Religion

The weights and the scales become irrelevant at the cross. God doesn't ask us to show up to Him with our evidence, our list, our scales, our pendulum swinging out of control. He doesn't ask for how our day went, with an explanation of each mess up. He doesn't ask why we felt like a good mom or the better mom when some days, some moments show we clearly were not. He doesn't ask us to pull out our evidence list, why we are a good or bad mom. He simply says: "You are my daughter. PaI love you because you are mine. I don't love you because of your good or bad behavior. Your good behavior doesn't make me love you more and your bad behavior doesn't make me love you less. I just love you."

Living in the Light

The good news of the cross of Christ means we get to live transformed—we no longer have to hide, skirting in and among the shadows, lurking. We can live in the light—full well knowing our mess ups and full well knowing we don't have to be defined by them because of what Jesus did. Yes, we will still fight the battles of fear, worry, anxiety, anger, rage, broken relationship, addiction, disease, and more every day. But, in that fight, we know there is HOPE at the end. There is HOPE in the moments of the battle.

Man, I needed God in deployment. His love for me and my need for Him was made abundantly clear. But the truth is, I need

God outside of deployment too. Deployment just brought me to my scraped knees, my scarcities and shortfalls in plain sight, the abundance of God's love wrapping my lack in His plenty. The HOPE of the Gospel changes everything. I no longer have to measure myself in the scales of good and bad behavior as a wife, mother, sister, friend, employee.

A question I found myself asking often in writing this book is: What do we keep in and what do we show others and why? What masks do we put on? How do we view ourselves before God? Deployment tested me in that it tested my transparency— What did I tell people when they asked how it was going vs. how was it really going? What did I tell God?

The good news of the Gospel is that we don't have to hide or feel shame before God or before others. We can be, just be. We can come to Him, just as we are, all of our mistakes and burdens and sins. God knows how it's really going. We can take off the mask of feeling like we have to have it together. We can talk to God, unhindered and unshackled, no mask, free to build relationships as a son or daughter of a Father who loves us. We can hang weightless at the pendulum, swinging no longer, the push to either side no longer necessary, the burden of pride and insecurity gone, held, home.

TWENTY-FOUR

YOU ARE LOVED, DEAR READER

To you, dear reader, I hope you have found something you can take with you here. I hope you take deep, long breaths; I hope you take it day by day, I hope you see that others care and that others have been down in the valley with you. I hope that the hardest of the hard days grants you wisdom to fully immerse yourself in the beauty of the sweetest of sweet days. I hope that the simple daily mediocrity of the tasks you do each day are made glorious in the revelation that this journey and these memories and the lessons you gain make you a more complete, more knowing, more compassionate, more loving relationship seeker, truth gatherer, supporter of American sacrifice and American freedom in all forms and a supporter of your own dreams, desires, and design. I, along with many others, are walking this step-by-step with you. *One step, then another.* You are loved, dear reader.

QUESTION GUIDE FOR INDIVIDUALS AND GROUPS

YES, I REMEMBER IT
Are there military spouses/partners/supporters that you know that you could interview?
What questions would you have for them?

INTERVIEW ONE: PRAYER AND OREOS
What activities do you enjoy doing with your loved one?
How could you incorporate that activity into deployment? (i.e., watching a certain show, reading a book, doing a workout plan together)

HIDDEN HAIR
What do "real life" military moments look like for you?
What moments have left you feeling frazzled?

INTERVIEW TWO: ONLY SNAIL MAIL
What relationships have you built with others whose loved ones are deployed?
How could you get more involved in getting to know others going through the same experiences as you?

ENTERING INTO OUR MESS

Have you ever let your worry of what others think of you keep you from having others over or from telling others "how it really is"?

What would it feel like or look like to invite others into your home even when things are a mess?

What would it feel like or look like to tell others "how it really is"? What's stopping you? How could you try to do this, even a little bit at a time?

INTERVIEW THREE: THE NORMAL LITTLE THINGS

This friend says: "A job shouldn't be our identity even if it is our own job but definitely don't find your identity in your significant other's job—be your own person outside of your job or your spouse's job".

Are there ways in which you have determined your identity or value based on your job?

Are there ways in which you have determined your identity or value based on your spouse's job?

In what ways can you "be your own person outside of your job or your spouse's job"?

WE MISSED HIM

What things will you miss most about your loved one when they are gone? Tell your loved one these things!

THE GIFT

Can you think of an example of a time when you put expectations on yourself or others that left you feeling frustrated?

How do expectations help us or hurt us?

INTERVIEW FOUR: THERE IS SO MUCH RICHNESS
This friend shares: "My husband and I are closer today and I am more like Jesus today. There is so much more richness. Because of COVID, my husband's deployment was extended. Instead of being bitter, I decided to use this time to take another trip to see a friend. I want to see the richness in God's provision."
In what ways can you see the richness in God's provision? What about during a time of deployment?
This friend shares: "You might say: 'Before we did this, can we try these different things?' You might say: 'These are hopes I have. These are fears I have.' Think about those things ahead of time."
If your partner has been gone before, what did you handle well as a couple?
What could you improve on this time?
What fears do you have?
What hopes do you have?

SWEET PEA
What losses or grief have you experienced?
How did it impact you?
How did you grow or learn from it?

THE BIRTH STORY
"We are all capable of so much more than we realize."
How could this be true for you?
What have you accomplished because of military life and deployment that has made you see your strength and ability?

INTERVIEW FIVE: DON'T STUFF FEELINGS
How is your experience in military life different or similar to this interview?

How has technology changed and in what way can you use technology to help you and your family communicate?

HELP
How have you been truly helped by others?
Have you ever been let down by someone's lack of offer of help?
What can you learn from this?
How can you help others more efficiently?
Is it hard for you to ask for help?
If so, why?
What emotional barriers might be in the way of you asking for help from others?

THE MELTING PLACE
What is your loved one going through?
Do you know their job and the hardships and highlights of it?
What struggles or hurts might they be going through?
How could you show compassion for their experience?

CREATIVE LOVE
What ways can you creatively love your significant other?
What things do you enjoy doing together that you could incorporate into your time away?
How can you tell and show your significant other that you love them and the things you love about them?

INTERVIEW SIX: JUST FLOAT
How could you view deployment as not time wasted but time gained?
In what ways can you flip your thinking upside down to see the best things deployment can bring?

How has deployment or difficult times in the military been used for the good in your life or in the life of others?
How can the time of deployment be redeemed?

UNEXPLAINED
What are you thankful for even during deployment or difficult seasons of military life?

THERE IS NO ONE MILITARY EXPERIENCE
What is your unique military story and experience?
How is it similar to or different from others that you know?

THE CORN MAZE
What are some unhealthy "repeat phrases" that could be turned into healthier thinking?

THE ONE STEP
What tool stood out to you as a practical next step?
What little hacks help you?

THE PENDULUM
How could you prepare for your loved one's return home?
If you are a parent, can you relate to the pendulum swing? How so?

THE RIVER
What is your own spiritual journey?
How might this help you through deployment?

THE LIGHT
How does it change the way you view God to know He doesn't determine His love for you based on your performance?

RESOURCES

INTERVIEW ONE: PRAYER AND OREOS
Instapaper. https://instapaper.com.

INTERVIEW FOUR: THERE IS SO MUCH RICHNESS
Daddy Dolls. https://hugahero.com.
Hagerty, Sara. *Every Bitter Thing Is Sweet.* Zondervan: 2014.
Yerkovich, Milan, and Kay Yerkovich. *How We Love.* WaterBrook: 2017.

INTERVIEW FIVE: DON'T STUFF FEELINGS
Elaine, Brye. *Be Safe, Love Mom.* Public Affairs: 2015.

INTERVIEW SIX: FRIEND THE RANDOM PERSON
Concrete Conversations. https://concrete-conversations.com.
Ehrmantraut, Brenda. *Night Catch.* Elva Resa Pub: 2014.
Franklin, Jesse, and Tahna Desmond Fox. *My Daddy Sleeps Everywhere.* Lionheart Group Publishing: 2017.
Otter, Isabel. *My Daddy Is A Hero.* Kane Miller: 2018.
Parker, Majorie Blain. *I Love You Near and Far.* Sterling Publishing Incorporated: 2015.
"Recordable Heart Plush | Hallmark." Hallmark Greeting Cards, Gifts, Ornaments, Home Decor & Gift Wrap | Hallmark.

https://www.hallmark.com/gifts/stuffed-animals/interactive-stuffed-animals/heart-recordable-plush-1PSB1046.html

"Recordable Storybooks | Hallmark." Hallmark Greeting Cards, Gifts, Ornaments, Home Decor & Gift Wrap | Hallmark. https://www.hallmark.com/gifts/books/recordable-story-books/

The Enneagram Institute. https://www.enneagraminstitute.com.

Wingate, M. C. *Emma the MEDEVAC Pilot*. Lightning Source Inc: 2019.

THE CORN MAZE

Ellis, A., and Joffe–Ellis, D. *Rational Emotive Behavior Therapy*, first edition. Washington, DC, American Psychological Association: 2011.

Boyes, A. "Cognitive Behavioral Therapy Techniques That Work: Mix and Match Cognitive Behavioral Therapy Techniques to Fit Your Preferences. *Psychology Today* (December 6, 2012). https://www.psychologytoday.com/blog/in-practice/201212/cognitive-behavioral-therapy-techniques-work.

Deffenbacher, J. L. (2011). "Cognitive–Behavioral Conceptualization and Treatment of Anger." *Cognitive and Behavioral Practice*, 18(2): 212–221.

ACKNOWLEDGMENTS

My sister was the first one who encouraged me to write a book specifically for those experiencing military life. Without her spark and push to keep going, this book wouldn't be here. Thank you for the million ways I could never name that you offered me encouragement and hope and took care of me. Thank you for all the ways you let me be just me. I love you sis.

My husband continues to support me. When I wanted to give up or thought what I had to say was not of value, he reminded me of truth. He did the hard work of giving me time away to be able to put these thoughts into words. I am forever thankful and in love with him.

To my mama, your love is the reason I am who I am today. You have been through the pits of the worst of the worst and back and you keep loving others every day. You have supported me through the ups and downs of my writing and my life, a consistent ear to listen to my woes. Thank you for loving me. Thank you for being an example to me of never giving up. I am proud to be your daughter.

To my Aunt Barb and Uncle Tony who came to be with us while my husband was gone, to my church family for the endless love, accountability, childcare, meals, and needed words of love, to dear friends and family who let me vent and cry and process in front of them, to the many others who cared deeply for me and my family, thank you. Thank you for all the little things you did that kept us going during deployment. We were lifted and pieced together because of you.

Special thanks to my counselor, Beth, for her gentle care and guidance. Thank you to the team at New Harbor Press for your patience and guidance and for helping this dream of a book become reality.

To my dear friends who allowed me to interview them: your bravery floored me. I am nowhere near the depth of women these ladies are and I am beyond grateful that each of them allowed me to pick their brain to share with you. Their vulnerability and willingness to share makes up the bulk of this book—their words are the substance.

ABOUT THE AUTHOR

Anna Luiken was born and raised in Wichita Falls, Texas, the home of dried grass and dear friends. She graduated with a degree in Interdisciplinary Studies with a focus on teaching middle school from Texas A&M University in 2011 and completed her Masters in Counseling from Wayland Baptist University in 2018. She has worked as a middle school science teacher, social worker in child protection, and now as a counselor serving at a residential and outpatient treatment center running individual, family, and group therapy sessions. She is passionate about hiking, hazelnut coffee, travel, facing your fears, making the important things important, knowing and loving your Creator, and family time.

CONTACT

If I can direct you, guide you, or help in any way, feel free to reach out. I would love to hear from you. My heart is with my readers.

Instagram: @annaluikenwriter
Website: annaluiken.com
Twitter: @annamluiken
Facebook Page: Anna Luiken Writer
Email: anna@annaluiken.com

CPSIA information can be obtained
at www.ICGtesting.com
Printed in the USA
LVHW041555280722
724609LV00003B/25